"T.J. Cloutier is probably the premier tournament player in the world today."

>Doyle "Texas Dolly" Brunson, two-time World Champion of Poker; author of *Super System* and *Super System 2*

"If there is one player that all of us fear the most at the final table, it is T.J. Cloutier."

>*Berry Johnston, 1986 World Champion of Poker*

"Tom McEvoy and T.J. Cloutier are an awesome team of hold'em players and writers. Now they have put their heads together and come up with the bible on no-limit and pot-limit hold'em."

>*Phil Hellmuth, 1989 World Champion of Poker*

"Tom McEvoy's tournament advice is the best ever written."

>*Barbara Enright, 1996 World Champion Pot-Limit Hold'em*

"T.J. is the best no-limit player on the tournament circuit today."

>*Hans "Tuna" Lund, 1996 World Champion Ace-to-5 Lowball*

"T.J. Cloutier is the number one no-limit poker player in the world. He and Tom McEvoy have written a book that is very much needed, but I think they may be giving away too much in *Championship No-Limit an*

>*Mansour*

CHAMPIONSHIP

NO-LIMIT HOLD'EM

and Pot-Limit Hold'em

T.J. CLOUTIER & TOM McEVOY

NO-LIMIT HOLD'EM

and Pot-Limit Hold'em

T.J. CLOUTIER & TOM McEVOY

CARDOZA PUBLISHING

Cardoza Publishing is the foremost gaming publisher in the world with a library of more than 200 up-to-date and easy-to-read books and strategies. These authoritative works are written by the top experts in their fields and with more than 10,000,000 books in print, represent the most popular gaming books anywhere.

NEW EDITION

First Printing   November 2009

Copyright© 1997, 2004, 2009 by T.J. Cloutier, Tom McEvoy &
Dana Smith
All Rights Reserved

ISBN 13: 978-1-5804-2258-1
ISBN 10: 1-58042-258-6

Library of Congress Control Number: 2008940743

Visit our website or write for a full list of Cardoza Publishing books
and advanced strategies.

CARDOZA PUBLISHING
P.O. Box 98115, Las Vegas, NV 89193
Toll-Free Phone (800)577-WINS
email: cardozabooks@aol.com
www.cardozabooks.com

ABOUT THE AUTHORS

T.J. Cloutier was inducted into the Poker Hall of Fame in 2006. He won the Player of the Year award in 1998 and 2002, and is considered to be one of the best tournament players in the world. Cloutier has won six World Series of Poker bracelets, and has appeared at the final table of the WSOP Main Event a remarkable four times, placing second in 1985 and in 2000. Overall, he has won more titles in no-limit and pot-limit hold'em than any other tournament player in the history of poker. Cloutier is the author of *How to Win the Championship*, and the co-author (with Tom McEvoy) of *Championship No-Limit & Pot-Limit Hold'em*, *Championship Omaha*, *Championship Hold'em* and *Championship Tournament Practice Hands*.

Tom McEvoy, the "Champion of Champions" has one of the most storied tournament careers of any poker player in history. In addition to winning four WSOP gold bracelets including the Main Event championship in 1983, McEvoy won the inaugural Champion of Champions tournament at the 2009 World Series of Poker in competition against the other living winners of the World Championship of Poker. He also won the 2005 Professional Poker Tour tournament sponsored by the World Poker Tour—an exclusive invitation-only event featuring the best players in the world—becoming the first player ever to win a PPT championship *and* a WSOP main event championship. A pioneer in improving conditions for poker players by sponsoring the nonsmoking movement in poker venues, McEvoy is the author and co-author of more than twelve other titles.

Though both T.J. Cloutier and Tom McEvoy worked together as co-authors for all sections of this book, T.J. took the role of lead author. Therefore, the "I" in each chapter is the speaking voice of T.J., except in chapters 2, 12, and 17 in which Tom is bylined as the lead author.

TABLE OF CONTENTS

3. 12 POWERFUL FACTORS THAT IMPACT TOURNAMENT SUCCESS   61

14. HOW TO BUILD THE POT ON THE FLOP IN POT-LIMIT   249

18. T.J.'S TALES FROM TEXAS 299

19. A CONVERSATION WITH HALL OF FAMER, T.J. CLOUTIER 317

GLOSSARY 333

FOREWORD

Mansour Matloubi, 1990 World Series of Poker Champion

T.J. Cloutier and Tom McEvoy have written a book that is very much needed by poker players. They may be giving too much away in *Championship No-Limit Hold'em and Pot-Limit Hold'em*, but that's okay with me! In fact, I was very surprised when T. J. told me that he and Tom were writing this book because in the past, there have been times at the poker table when I would say something to another player that I thought might help him, and T.J. would go ballistic about not wanting to "educate" the opposition. I am very glad that he has changed his mind.

All of the top poker players think that if they get lucky, they are unbeatable. But during the World Series of Poker, or in any other big no-limit tournament, if there is any player in the world that I would like to trade a piece with, it is T. J. Cloutier. When I first met him in 1989 in Malta, it was the first time that he had ever played against Europeans. After just a few hours of play, he basically knew everything about everybody who played poker in Europe. All he had to do was play you for a few hands and he knew exactly what you were made of and who was capable of doing what.

He sits in a tournament and moves from one table to another table and he soon knows every poker player in the world; and if he doesn't, he will find out in a few minutes, quicker than anybody else that I know. Sometimes, I can't figure people out as quickly as he does, but the way that he plays them is a good enough example for me to follow. I have never seen anybody so strong. We played head-up at the Diamond Jim Brady tournament in 1990 just after I had won the World Series of Poker. I was running good at the final table, making hands, betting and raising. But I never bluffed because, basically, I didn't need to. When the final hand came up, T.J. had a small pair and a flush draw, 7♥ 3♥. My hand was the 6♥ 9♥. Two overcards were on the board. There was no movement to this pot until the turn. A 7 came on the turn, which gave T.J. a pair and gave me a straight draw. The river card was another overcard. He checked it and I bet all my chips. It was the first time at the final table that I had bluffed at the pot. With no hesitation, he called me with two sevens. No other player in the world would have done that! Later, we were joking about it.

This was the last $10,000 tournament at the Diamond Jim Brady; the first prize was $250,000 and second place was $160,000. There hadn't been a deal—we were playing for it all. How could this guy have read his opponent like that? I will never forget that hand, and I have told him many times that he made the greatest play that I have ever seen. He is the only player in the world that is capable of calling a pot like that. I think that T.J. is the best psychologist in the world!

Some of us might miss things at the poker table. We get involved in conversation and other things that are going on. But it seems to me that when T. J. is involved in con-versation at the table, he still isn't missing a thing. Somehow, as he is talking, he is still playing his opponents correctly. It comes so naturally to him. I think the rest of us have to work hard at it. Sometimes, when we are making decisions about calling or not calling, we think about it for a few minutes and then might change our minds. But T.J.'s decisions are based on his first instinct. The first thing that crosses his mind is his last action. He acts more quickly than anyone else I know.

Tom McEvoy and I are more logical, mathematical and theoretical in our style. Basically, we are looking more at the value of the hand than the value of the opponent and that has been successful for us. T. J. would rather play his opponents than his cards. His emphasis is more on his opponents, picking his spots at the poker table, whereas Tom prefers to have the best hand. In this respect, I think that T. J. and Tom have the best partnership in writing this book. Tom writes the more theoretical part and T. J. does the more psychological aspects of the book. I think that they are waking up the senses of people with the writing of this book. The first time that you read a book, it may not have an impact upon you. But over time, you become aware of the things that the authors are talking about. Probably, when T. J. was learning poker, there was no book to help him. But now, he and Tom are bringing their winning ideas to you. And in the end, this book will make a big difference.

T. J. has not won the World Series no-limit title yet, but in my opinion, he is the most deserving person to win it in the future. He is head and shoulders above anyone else. He is a legend. I believe that, by far, he is the number-one no-limit poker player in the world.

INTRODUCTION

Tom McEvoy,
1983 World Series of
Poker Champion

T. J. Cloutier and I first began talking about writing a poker book together several years ago, but we weren't sure exactly what type of book we should write. Between the two of us, we have won ten World Series of Poker titles and more than 100 other major titles in games ranging from razz to no-limit hold'em. In fact, T. J. holds more titles in pot-limit and no-limit hold'em than any other player in the world. After researching the books available on today's market, we decided that a manual that would help people learn how to win at no-limit and pot-limit hold'em would be the most valuable contribution that we could make. *Championship No-Limit and Pot-Limit Hold'em* is our way of giving something back to the world of poker, a world that has given both of us so much pleasure, excitement, and income over the past three decades.

We also believe that this book will help to build the ranks of no-limit and pot-limit hold'em players. These are exciting poker games, games filled with intrigue, games that require an above average amount of skill. Some players are afraid to try playing them—they don't know how, or they may be afraid of the big-bet aspect of them, or maybe the "big" players that they think they will have to compete against in tournaments.

If you have been wanting to learn how to play no-limit or pot-limit hold'em but have been reluctant to try playing them for any of these reasons, throw your reservations out the window and dig into *Championship No-Limit and Pot-Limit Hold'em*—we wrote this book for you.

We don't use any fancy language and we leave no gaps in explaining how you can win. Our editor, Dana Smith, tells me that we aren't boring, either. T. J. discusses how to play no-limit and pot-limit in the same way that he talks—in that good ol' Texas poker player lingo that everybody who has ever heard him speak agrees is colorful, simple, and brilliant. He even allows me to make an occasional comment about the play of a hand. In fact we have made it a point to give you our different views on strategy because we think that you deserve to know that not everybody agrees on exactly how to play poker.

We also include plenty of hand illustrations to let you see what you are reading, to visualize yourself in a particular scenario, and to analyze how you would play in different situations. T. J. tells you how hands have been played in actual games at the World Series of Poker, in Texas, and in California. I don't think he's ever forgotten a hand he's played or a face he has seen or the playing style of anybody he has played against. His memory is incredible and his talent is awesome.

We have tried to bring you T.J.'s vast reservoir of experience and expertise in games that he learned as a road gambler in Texas. He is a seasoned veteran who has earned his stripes on battle fields ranging from dingy backroom games to the glitz and glamour of the World Series of Poker. I am proud to be a friend of T.J.'s and I am proud of this book that we have created together. And I also am happy that he was inducted into the Poker Hall of Fame in 2006, an honor he truly deserves.

This revised and updated edition of *Championship No-Limit & Pot-Limit Hold'em* includes new topics and added strategies to more fully educate you in how to win against today's more sophisticated cash-game and tournament players. With the knowledge that you have learned from this updated version of the trusted advice we gave you in our first edition—and a little bit of experience under your belt—I am confident that we will meet one day soon in the winners' circle.

THE 10 MOST VALUABLE SKILLS IN BIG-BET POKER

From 1981 until 1992, I played no-limit hold'em in Dallas from noon until 5:00 p.m. every Monday through Friday, and from 7:00 p.m. to midnight or later five days a week. On Sundays, I drove to Shreveport to play pot-limit hold'em. I was putting in sixty hours a week, and sometimes eighty, playing no-limit and pot-limit poker during those eleven years. Players used to come from all over the nation to play in our game at a place that we will call The Big Texan's. His house had the best food and the cleanest environment you could ask for, and it was a safe game, too.

All the road gamblers came to play in the game—Willie Struthers, Berry Johnston and Steve Melvin drove in from Oklahoma City, Garland Walters came in from Kentucky, Gene Fisher from El Paso, Bobby Baldwin from Tulsa, Buddy Williams, all the best players. That game was a great training ground in no-limit hold'em. Tom told me, "I lost about $15,000 playing no-limit hold'em in that game, but I won $40,000 at pot-limit Omaha. Until then, I thought I was a no-limit hold'em player—boy, did I learn a few lessons! People that I'd never heard of before were some of the best players that I had ever seen."

The Big Texan was a whale of a man and he ran the best game in Dallas. But he was one of the most disliked men there, too. I'm a very calm person, but there were three times in those eleven years when I almost stood up and let him have it. I didn't because I knew that this was a game in which I could make a lot of money and I wasn't going to get shut out of it. One night we were playing no-limit hold'em and I raised the pot $200 with A-Q suited. The Big Texan called it. It got around to Walter Jones, and he put in his last $400. This was a legal raise because the raise in no-limit hold'em has to be double the amount of the original raise. I decided I was going to shut the Big Texan out of the pot so I came back over the top with $2,000 to get head-up with Jones.

"That's not a raise," the Big Texan said.

"The hell if it's not," I answered. "It's as legal as it can be."

Everybody at the table was agreeing with me, when the Big Texan just reached over and slapped me on the hand. Well, I reared up and I was really going to let him have it because I never cared for him one iota anyway. But I thought better of it because I needed that game; it paid all my expenses for the year. Of course, the raise stood and he threw his hand away. He told me later that if I had hit him, he would've gone for his gun. "Buddy," I said, "if I had hit you, you'd never have had a chance to get that gun out."

The Big Texan was always afraid that the money would leave Dallas. When I was still just dating my wife Joy, he called her and said, "How come you let T. J. go out to those tournaments? Don't you know that he could lose all his money in those things?" He's the same one that said he was going to drop the latch on me after I'd won twelve times in a row in his game. "You're beating these boys too bad," he said, "and I don't want that money going back to Louisiana. But if you'll let me have half of your play, you can keep on playing here."

So for the next eleven games, the Big Texan was in on my action and we won all eleven times. On the twelfth night, he said, "I'm out today." That was just like a bell going off in my head; I knew that something was going to go down in the game that day. There were a few strangers from Oklahoma in the game that I'd never seen before. So I just bought in for $500 instead of the usual $1,000, played for about an hour, and left. And the Big Texan never came in with me again.

There were a ton of good players in Dallas. In fact, if you could beat the Dallas game, you could beat any game, including the World Series of Poker. You see, the World Series is a conglomeration of local champions. There's Joe Blow from Iowa who's the champion in his game at home; hundreds of local champions like him come to Vegas to play the World Series. But it's like the difference in going from playing high school football to college football: It's a big step up. And then going from college to pro football is the next big step.

It's not a question of whether these players can play poker—they just can't play it on the level that some of the top players can. It's similar to Tiger Woods. There are a lot of great golfers out there right now, but Tiger Woods is *the* golfer, the one with the most talent. There is a lot of skill difference among poker pros, too. The top pros have a higher skill level, one that they have developed over a long period of time.

Here are the ten most valuable skills you need to develop to join the pros in the big leagues.

1. CONSTANTLY OBSERVE YOUR OPPONENTS

Knowing your opponents in pot-limit and no-limit hold'em is the most important skill to learn if you want to be successful at big-bet poker. I once took a friend who didn't play much poker to a game with me. He saw us talking when we were out of a hand, and then he noticed me talking to a guy across the table while a hand was being played.

"How can you tell what's going on if you're talking?" he asked me.

"If a wing fell off a gnat at the end of the table, I'd see it," I answered.

"No matter what's going on at the same time?"

"That's right. In this game you have to be alert at all times, even when you're not playing a hand."

If you want to be successful at pot-limit or no-limit hold'em, you've gotta' be able to sit down at a table with eight or nine people that you've never played with in your life, and after ten or fifteen minutes, know how each one of them plays—whether they're aggressive; whether they're passive; how they play early position, middle position, late position. You have to get an initial line on their play.

We're just like leopards: We can't change our spots. A man who used to play with us in Texas years ago would play as good a poker game as anybody I'd ever seen play—for the first two hours. You could've put a stopwatch on him. He'd hit a stone wall after two hours and then his whole game would revert back to the way he always played. He would start bluffing in bad spots, and started giving his money away. With a player like that, you can just wait on him. You know he's going to crumble in two hours, so wait him out. You're going to win the money. I might forget a person's name, but I'll never forget his face or how he plays in all situations, no matter if I've only played with him one time in my life. The main thing is being very observant and watching what players do in different situations.

If a player has raised before the flop with A-K and the flop comes with three babies, is he the type of player who will lead with this hand? Or is he the type of player who will check his

A-K because he doesn't have anything yet? Suppose somebody else bets when the baby flop hits, and he calls. What does that tell you? It tells me that he has committed a mortal sin in poker. If you don't flop to it, get rid of your hand. But you see pot-limit and no-limit players who call in this situation all the time, especially when you're playing against people who are used to playing limit hold'em. They're going to bet A-K against a board with three babies, or they're going to call with A-K. But you always have an edge on them if you know how they play in that spot.

Observe your opponents as the cards are being dealt. As people are making bets, always look at the people in front of and behind you. I don't wait for the action to get to me before I look at my hand, I look at my cards when I first get them so that I can observe the other players. If you're looking at your hand when the action gets to you rather than looking at the people behind you, you're missing a lot. It's the old "load-up" theory. A lot of poker players can't stand the thrill when they pick up a big hand. In their anticipation of a win, they load up their hands with chips before it's their turn to act. If you're observant, you'll fold a mediocre hand because you know that the guy behind you is going to raise. It happens many, many times.

2. DETERMINE WHO IS OVERLY AGGRESSIVE

Some players are overly aggressive, especially in today's fast games. If you watch them very carefully, you will find that they can't stand two checks. So if you have a big hand, you can check to them *twice*. Let them eat themselves up. Even some of the legendary players who have had a lot of success on the circuit can't stand two checks and you can trap some of these big-name players by just checking it to them two times. Some of the really aggressive players such as the late Stu Ungar fit into this category.

In tournament poker, you can come over the top of these aggressive players. You know their level of tolerance, that they can't stand two checks. You don't even need a hand to win the pot! All you need to do is play back against them on fourth street. When you're running good, they'll throw their hands away every time. And then the one time that you really have a hand and make this play, that's the time when they'll call you. Timing is everything in poker.

One of the main concepts in pot-limit and no-limit is that there are situations when you don't need to have a hand to win a good pot, whereas in limit hold'em, you have to show down a hand almost every time.

3. KEEP A BOOK

I have almost a photographic memory about situations in poker, so I don't need to go home and write things down, but I think that it's a good practice for most players. After your session, go home and think about the game and the players. During an eight-hour session, thirty to forty key hands will be played. You should be able to remember these hands. Keep a little book on all the players, what they did in these key hands, because they're going to do the same thing the next time you play them. And you're going to be the recipient of their generosity, of their playing patterns.

For example, I know a player who will always bring it in for a small raise when everybody has passed to him on the button; he never comes in flat. And he's a good enough player that he doesn't stand a reraise unless he has a big hand. Knowing that he plays very aggressively off the button, you can make a lot of money from this man when you're in the little blind or the big blind by just popping him back three or four times in a session. Obviously, if you do it every time, you're going to get yourself killed, but you can tell when to do it.

When you're playing nine-handed and six players have passed to you on the button, with eighteen cards already dealt out, there's a pretty good chance that somebody behind you might have a hand since nobody in front of you does. Tom calls that "the bunching factor." It doesn't necessarily have to work that way, but it seems reasonable to assume that if everybody has passed, it is more likely than usual that the blinds, or possibly the button, could have a legitimate hand.

Remember that when you're on the button, you're in the power position. The blinds will always have to act before you do after the flop. A lot of times, you don't have to make that button raise. If you just call, they will have to come to you. And when they have to come to you, that gives you all the options in the world after you've seen the flop. Contrary to what a lot of players do, I limp on the button quite often, unless I have a big hand. Many players in tournaments get into the habit of raising on the button with no hand to pick up the blinds. I'm not always on the button when I try to steal. Sometimes, I might make a play from the cutoff seat, one in front of the button.

In a tournament I recently played, a player had raised on the button against my big blind about ten straight times. Three times, I had gone over the top of him. In this particular hand, he came in for a small raise when I had A-J in the big blind. I knew that this man was going to make a move on me, he's that type of player. I had played with him before and remembered him. So, I raised him. Then he says, "I'm moving all in." All

I had was A-J, but I knew that I had the best hand. And sure enough, I did. He had 9-6 offsuit. He got lucky and won the pot when he flopped two nines, but that's not the point. The play was correct in the way that I had set it up.

4. LEARN HOW TO SET UP PLAYS

Pot-limit and no-limit hold'em are games in which you can set up plays. At Vegas World years ago, I was watching "Joe Dokes" play. Since then, Joe has turned into a very decent player and has finished high in a lot of tournaments, but this incident happened when he first started on the poker scene. It was passed to me on the button and I made a play at the pot with A-7 offsuit because the blinds were pretty good sized. Joe reraised me from the big blind. I had more chips than he had, and I knew that there was only one hand that he could have that he would call me with if I moved in on him over the top for the third raise. He would have to have aces. Seeing that I had an ace, I made the play and went all-in on him. Joe had two kings, but he threw them away. Then I showed him the A-7. For a purpose.

About thirty-five minutes later, I had two sevens on the button. It was passed to me and I made a slight raise. Joe called and I knew that he was trying to trap me by the way that he acted when he called. He screwed up to the table and made a few moves that I had observed before. The flop came 7-4-2.

T.J.　　　　　　　**JOE**

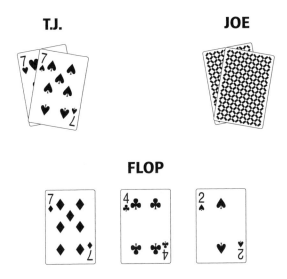

FLOP

He checked to me, I bet, and he beat me to the pot moving in. He had a big pair and I ate him alive with the trip sevens. Joe got trapped because of the A-7 that I had showed him previously. You see, one play can set up another play, and you have to think this way all the time.

Of course, these types of plays are far more common in pot-limit and no-limit than they are in limit hold'em. I think that limit hold'em is a game that you have to play so much tighter than you play pot-limit and no-limit. It's much more technical, and you don't have many different moves. In limit hold'em, you have to show down a lot of hands.

Several good players that I know raise with some strange hands. For example, Phil Hellmuth raises with a few hands that I would never consider raising. And he calls with hands that I wouldn't call with. People looking on will say, "How could he make that play? And he wins with it!" But he has a reason for doing it. It all depends on who he's playing with and what he's trying to accomplish. When you get to the top rung of the ladder, the skill level is extremely high. You can set up players in no-limit, but you can't set them up very often in limit because it's so easy for them to call in limit poker that it literally limits your options.

5. BE CAREFUL WITH YOUR CALLS

A bettor be, a caller never. You have two chances at the pot by betting: Either your opponent will muck his hand, or you have the best hand. When you're calling, your chances are slim and none unless you've set things up for a call. In other words, you call for a particular reason, primarily because you've set up a play and you want your opponent to bet.

Don't ever become a calling station in pot-limit or no-limit hold'em. But when you do call, make sure that you have a good purpose. Say the flop comes 9-8-7. You have Q-J in your hand, you have a lot of chips in front of you, and so does your opponent.

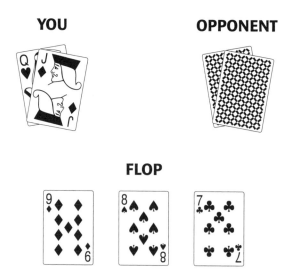

YOU
OPPONENT

FLOP

He makes a decent bet on the flop. There's nothing wrong with calling one time because you have two overcards and a straight draw. If you catch a 10 to make your straight on the turn, you'll have the nuts, and can play the hand many different ways in order to win a pretty good-sized pot. You don't make this play very often in no-limit, and certainly never when you have a short stack in a tournament. It always depends on your stack size compared to your opponent, and your pot odds.

6. WATCH FOR TELLS FROM YOUR OPPONENTS

Keep a book on everybody and you put in it the kinds of hands they play. McEvoy and I started playing together around 1979, and I'm sure that he knows what I do, and I know what he does, too. We've watched all the really good players over the years—and every one of them has a tell. Even legendary players like Stu Ungar and John Bonetti had tells. If you observe enough and watch them play hands for long enough, you'll find that everybody has a certain tell when they have a really *big* hand versus just a hand. Of course, the top players don't show tells very often, but they *do* show them from time to time.

For example, one top-notch tournament player has a way of betting his chips. He starts to make a call and then goes back to get more chips and says, "Raise." Every time this player makes that go-back move, he's there with a hand. Another player has a "hitch" move when he has a big hand. He'll come out with the amount that he's supposed to call with, hesitate out there with his hand, go back to his stack, and then come back out with a raise. Every time he does this, he has a big hand. If he doesn't do it, there's a bigger chance that he has a mediocre hand. In other words, if his move is more fluid, he usually doesn't have quite the strength that he is representing. These are fabulous things to know about your opponents.

And how do you get to know them? Only through observation.

7. KNOW YOUR OWN HABITS

One time when I was just starting out in poker, I caught myself in the habit of pushing my cards back into my chips whenever I had a big hand, instead of just leaving them out there. "Well," I thought after I had discovered my own tell, "maybe I can use this in reverse." So, one or two times during a game, I'd push my cards back toward my chips when I *didn't* have a hand. And boy, it worked! It confused the guys who'd been observing me and had picked up on my tell.

You have to know your own characteristics. How many times have you had the absolute nuts against an opponent who is a pretty loose player, and you want him to call you? And he starts icing you down, looking at you before he calls to see whether you have a tell or are giving any clues. At those times, I've swallowed hard and looked to the side, trying to induce him to call. This is one way that you can use some of your tells in *reverse* to your favor.

8. FOLLOW YOUR FIRST INSTINCT

Tom told me a story about second-guessing himself on a player's tell. "I was in there with a pretty weak hand, an A-5, which I had raised with from a middle position before the flop," he said. "I'd been catching some hands and my table image was strong. Freddy Deeb called my raise. The flop came J-J-5.

TOM

FREDDY

FLOP

I bet the flop and Deeb called. A nothing card came off on the turn and I checked. So did he. Another blank came on the river and I checked again. Then Freddy made a big bet at the pot. I looked at him and his hand was trembling.

"My first instinct was to muck my hand, but I thought he looked nervous and might be putting a play on me. I called—he turned up a J-6 suited. So, detecting nervousness doesn't necessarily mean weakness; it could mean strength, too. As it turns out, he was nervous that I might *not* call him!

"My gut instinct told me I should muck my cards. But trying to pick off the tell, I second-guessed myself." Happens to the best of us, I believe, when we don't trust our first instinct.

On these types of flops, if you have raised going in and your opponent called the raise, you probably don't have anything. He could have two sixes in the hole and have you beat. Once you make your little cursory bet at the pot, you're through with this hand if you get called. You're completely through with it: You cannot lose any more money to it, I don't care *what* your opponent has.

Your first instincts are better than 95 percent correct if you're a dedicated poker player. That's because your instincts come from all the training and practice and skills that you've learned over the years. What you think *after* your first instinct is the type of thinking that goes, "What hands can I beat?" You *never* think about what hands you can beat. "Do I have the best hand?" is what you should be thinking.

My wife Joy was sitting on the sidelines watching us play at Binion's in 1994 when I won the pot-limit hold'em tournament at the World Series of Poker. She heard the people around her asking, "What's happening? T.J.'s not playing any pots. He's got chips, but he's just sitting there." A fella who had watched me play a lot of tournaments said, "You watch what happens when they get down to three players. The big money's in the top three positions. Just watch him open up and get aggressive *then*."

And that's exactly what happened. When you're playing tournament poker, the money's in the top three spots and you've got to get there. Sure, you're going to play marginal hands sometimes, and you're going to play different situations. But you cannot do that all of the time. You have to use correct timing.

9. LEARN HOW TO ANALYZE PLAYERS CORRECTLY

Now let's analyze the play of a top-notch tournament player who has won some major titles. I'm going to call him "John Smith." Smith has a very big "sizz" potential. You can expect Smith to play very good poker unless he takes a very bad beat. Then he sizzles. When players like Smith get a very big hand beaten, what do they do during the next ten or fifteen minutes? That's when you look for the potential sizz, the tilt factor.

A lot of players become overly aggressive when they take a bad beat. They will play a hand that they shouldn't be in with, get a little flop to it, and then get it beat—and then they get even crazier. Smith often does this when he gets a hold of a lot of chips. He's a truly great player, but he has a bad habit of thinking that nobody else at the table can play. So, he thinks that because he makes a move at the pot, his opponents should automatically lose the pot to him. But it doesn't happen that way. Naturally, the time to get a jump on a player like Smith is during the ten or fifteen minutes after he takes the beat.

Any player should be able to take any kind of a beat and not let it change his style one iota. Over 10,000 or 100,000 hands, everybody is going to catch the same kinds of cards. It's how you play them that comes out in the wash.

When Smith breaks his chips down to call, he will turn them out in stacks of five or so, then he'll stack them up, and then he'll go back to the stack, then bring them back out and stack them up again. And he usually makes the call or a raise when he does this. When he goes back and forth with his chips, most of the time he has a big hand. And he usually cuts off his chips to the right. But every once in a while, I've seen him cut them off to the left. Now, when he stacks them reverse to his usual pattern, he's usually on a draw or a bluff. This is just an example of the things that you can observe in a poker game and use to your advantage.

Then there's the type of player who splashes his chips in front of him—he never stacks his chips, he just splashes them out toward the pot. Suppose he's been doing this all day long in your game. Then suddenly, he cuts his chips out and stacks them up very nicely. Now that's a big difference in his usual style. When he splashes his chips, does he have a hand or doesn't he have a hand, as opposed to what he has when he stacks them out neatly?

If you've been watching him, you'll know. Yu've learned something about this player—which way he has a hand, and which way he doesn't have one, or whether the way he puts in his chips means anything at all. It may not, but usually it does.

10. ALWAYS PLAY YOUR A-GAME

People always revert back to their own styles. A lot of players in a tournament play their A-games for an hour or so, until they can't stand it any longer. Then they all go back to their natural style of play. Maybe they've been trying to play real snug or real solid, whatever they think their A-game is. Some of the better players may even hold out for two hours. Of course, we're not talking about the great players who get the money most of the time in tournaments.

There are a lot of players in tournaments who don't have an A-game. These players can be very dangerous because anybody can pick up two cards and get a flop to them. But in the long run, the weaker players are going to make calls and plays that are so far out of line that they don't have a chance to win the tournament.

Every now and then, somebody will come along like the late Hal Fowler, the first amateur ever to win the championship. It was one of the biggest upset in the history of poker when he won the World Series in 1979. He made four or five inside straights at the final table—three of them against the great Bobby Hoff when they were playing head-up. You could've played as good as God can play, and you couldn't have won those pots. You can't win a tournament when a player is doing that to you for a big amount of money.

But regardless of these types of amazing things that occasionally happen, still play your A-game and maintain your observation powers. Knowing how the other people play in various situations with different hands, and keeping that book on everybody are so important that I can't say it often enough. Observation is the strongest tool in pot-limit and no-limit poker.

In the next chapter, Tom McEvoy lists ten specific skills you can use in no-limit hold'em cash games and tournaments. These skills are an integral part of every top player's A-game.

TOP 10 TIPS FOR WINNING AT NO-LIMIT HOLD'EM

Tom McEvoy

Playing your A-game all the time in every cash game or tournament you enter often turns out to be more of a goal than a reality. To turn your goals into reality requires constant attention to the details as well as the big picture.

No-limit hold'em has replaced limit hold'em as the king of poker games. A few years ago there were far more limit than no-limit hold'em games in walk-in casinos and Internet sites. The reverse is now true, especially on the tournament scene.

Cash games with $1/$2, $1/$3, and $2/$5 blinds are quite common in walk-in casinos. At online sites, the small blind is almost always exactly one-half the size of the big blind. You can play much smaller games online than in walk-in casinos, with blinds as small as 25¢/50¢ and limits as low as 1¢/2¢.

When playing small games online or in a casino, you can expect a lot more people to see the flop. Limping occurs far more frequently and multiway flops are the norm rather than the exception. Even when the pot gets raised preflop, a lot of players are usually willing to gamble. They seem to like building a bigger pot to shoot for, and having one or two players call the raise up front, seems to attract even more players into the pot.

Bluffing in these smaller games is highly overrated. People will look you up with second pair or even bottom pair, so be very careful about who you try to bluff. In fact, we recommend taking the bluff right out of your game for the most part. If you do decide to bluff, make sure it's against an opponent who is capable of making a laydown rather than someone who will automatically call you with any kind of marginal hand.

When you get a big starting hand like A-A, K-K or Q-Q, try to limit the number of players in the pot. A decent sized raise is the only way to do that. If somebody has already raised in front of you, reraise to get it heads-up. Slow playing is a good way to get your big pair cracked because it often allows other players to see the flop cheaply.

In summary, see flops with marginal hands cheaply, especially in position; don't slow-play, and seldom bluff. Small no-limit hold'em games require a lot of patience and the ability to handle frustration, because with more players involved in each pot, you will be drawn out on more often.

Here are my best tips for turning your dreams into dollars at no-limit hold'em. I have adapted them from *Beat Texas Hold'em*, a book I wrote with Shane Smith.

1. BIG PAIRS AND HIGH CARDS ARE THE BOSS HANDS IN NO-LIMIT HOLD'EM

No-limit hold'em is a game of big cards. Playing small pairs and medium suited connectors is simply too expensive unless you can play them cheaply from late position. The five best starting hands are aces, kings, queens, A-K and jacks. You usually can play these hands for a raise from any position.

Just remember that A-K, even suited, is still a drawing hand, not a made hand. You will usually have to flop something to A-K to make it profitable to continue playing after the flop.

Any pair lower than aces can get you into trouble before the flop if you don't play it properly. If someone is willing to put a lot of money in the pot preflop, even a high pair could be in trouble.

If nobody has entered the pot and I am sitting in the cutoff seat or the button, I will usually raise with any hand that has two cards 10 or higher in it. This means that, in addition to the top five starting hands, hands like J-10, Q-10, A-J, A-10, K-J, K-Q, K-10, A-Q and pocket tens become raising hands from a late position. If someone reraises me, I will have to decide whether to continue playing or fold.

CUTOFF SEAT AND BUTTON

Raising Hands in Pots No One Has Entered

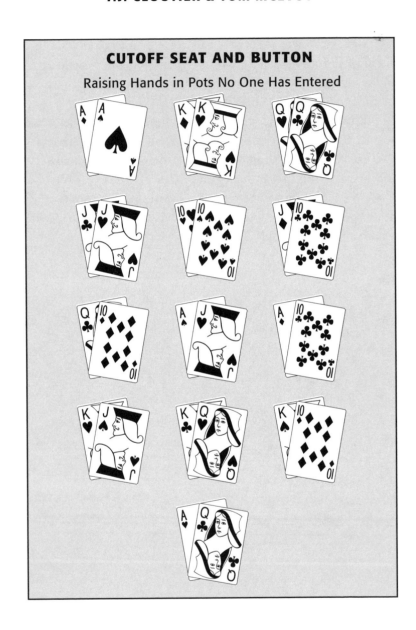

2. PLAY FEWER HANDS THAN YOU WOULD PLAY IN LIMIT HOLD'EM

To be a successful no-limit hold'em player, you don't need to play a lot of hands, but you do need to win the majority of the hands you decide to play. Many hands that play reasonably well in limit hold'em—hands such as A-Q, K-J suited, pocket tens and suited connectors in multiway pots—do not play nearly as well in no-limit hold'em.

The reason that these marginal hands don't do very well in no-limit hold'em is because your opponent can make a big enough bet to make it unprofitable to continue playing the hand. In limit hold'em, where you and your opponents are restricted to a limited number of fixed bets and raises, you usually do not have to put your entire stack of chips in jeopardy on any one hand. Because you can lose all your chips on one hand, cards like the A-Q and K-J that I mentioned can be extremely troublesome and difficult to play in no-limit hold'em.

For example, suppose a player raises in early position and you are on the button with A-Q. You think to yourself, "I have two big cards and position on this raiser. I'll call him and see what develops." The flop comes A-10-5 rainbow (three different suits). Now you say to yourself, "This is okay, I have top pair with a pretty good kicker. Yummy!"

Your opponent, the one who raised in early position, checks to you. "I'm gonna make about a pot-sized bet here," you think. "I probably have the best hand, so I might as well bet and try to win some more of my opponent's money." You make the bet and your opponent studies you for a moment, staring at you intensely. Then he makes the exact announcement you didn't want to hear: "I'm raising all in!"

Now what do you do?

You're probably drawing to just three outs to win the pot, the three queens that are left in the deck. If you had been studying your opponent and had determined that he was a tight player, you probably should have folded your hand before the flop against his early-position raise.

This is just one example of the problems that can develop in the play of no-limit hold'em if you try to play the same types of hands you are accustomed to playing in limit hold'em. Where only a few extra bets could be in jeopardy when you play a mediocre hand in limit hold'em, your entire stack of chips can be ruined when you play marginal cards in no-limit hold'em.

3. LEARN HOW MUCH TO RAISE

One of the most common mistakes that new players make in no-limit hold'em is betting the wrong amount of chips when they raise. New players usually do one of two things—they either underbet the pot or they overbet it. Either of these mistakes can get you into trouble.

Underbetting the pot is a very common mistake that beginners make. Oftentimes I see several people enter the pot for the minimum bet, which is always the size of the big blind. Then someone in late position makes a raise exactly double the size of the big blind, a very weak play. Raising such a small amount won't drive any of the original callers out of the pot, and could give one of the early limpers an opportunity to make a much bigger raise, forcing everyone out of the pot.

Try this tactic instead: Simply call and see what develops after the flop. Having late position gives you the advantage on all future betting rounds.

Overbetting the pot is another common mistake. Suppose the blinds are $10/$25 and nobody has entered the pot yet.

You look down and find two beautiful aces, the best possible starting hand. You get excited, your heart starts beating faster and you announce, "I raise!" as you shove $500 into the pot. Everyone folds, including the blinds, and you have just won the pot. Winning the pot is good, of course, except for one minor detail—you have only made a $35 profit with the best possible starting hand.

What happened?

You made the mistake of overbetting the pot and forcing everyone out. If you had bet a little less—around $100—you might have gotten a caller and won a bigger pot. It's true that you could also have gotten outdrawn and lost with your aces, but that's a chance you must take. After all, you can't make an omelet without breaking a few eggs, and you can't be a winner at no-limit hold'em unless you can make the most profit out of your strong starting hands.

So, how much should you raise when you enter the pot in no-limit hold'em? As a general guideline, raise three to four times the size of the big blind. For example, if the big blind is $20, raise to $60 or $80.

4. PLAY VERY FEW HANDS FROM EARLY POSITION

The earlier your position in relation to the big blind, the worse it is for you. The later your position, the better it is for you. When you are the last player to act, you know what everybody is doing before the action gets to you. This is a big advantage. If you are the first to act, all the other players have an edge on you because you have to act on your hand before they do. This means that many hands that are playable in late position are not playable in early position.

If you enter the pot from early position with a drawing hand such as the 10♣ 9♣, for example, you don't know whether someone will raise after you enter the pot. This could make that type of hand too expensive to play for profit. Hands with middle-rank connecting cards need lots of callers and, preferably, no preflop raise to make them worthwhile playing.

Most players, even professional players, lose money by playing hands in the first two seats after the big blind. Only the best starting hands like big pairs and A-K can be played for a long-term profit from early position. Small pairs and suited connectors just do not play well from up front.

5. GET TO KNOW THE PLAYING STYLES OF YOUR OPPONENTS

Poker is a people game played with cards, not a card game played with people. This means that you need to learn how to play your cards against the different types of people you are likely to face at the poker table. You should always try to play your hand one way against a tight conservative player, and play your hand in a different way against a loose aggressive player.

For example, say that you have the A-J of clubs and are sitting on the button. Cobweb Carl, who has not played a hand in over an hour, raises from an early position. What kind of hand do you think he has? By his previous play, he has showed you that he doesn't play very many hands. Now he has cards he likes enough to raise with from an early position. I'd fold my hand in a New York minute against this type of player in this situation. I would be afraid that I was up against a big pair or A-K, which would make it very difficult for me to win the pot with a lesser hand.

Now let's say that you have the same hand and again you are the button. Everybody folds to Rammin' Robert on your immediate right (the cut-off seat) and he raises. In fact, Robert has raised the last three hands and has played over 50 percent of the hands dealt to him. What do you think of his raise?

I would reraise him. I probably have not only a better starting hand, I also have position on him. By reraising I can probably force the blinds to throw their hands away, an added bonus for raising, and get it heads-up between Robert and me.

The point is that against the tight player, I would fold, but against the loose player, I would raise. In other words I would play the very same hand totally differently depending upon the playing style of my opponent.

6. LEARN HOW TO BLUFF IN THE RIGHT SITUATIONS

The bluff is a major element in playing no-limit hold'em successfully. However, many new players make the classic mistake of bluffing too often, probably because they've been watching too many no-limit hold'em tournaments on TV. The World Poker Tour and the World Series of Poker bring all the top poker action right into your living room. What you are watching, however, is usually just the final-table action, not the preliminary play that helped the finalists to get there.

When the audience sees players raising each other with hands like 4-3, or moving all their chips into the center of the table with nothing but a flush draw, they think that's how to play the game. They're led to believe that players bluff far more often in no-limit hold'em that they actually do. The truth is that final-table action is quite a bit different from the play in the early stages of the tournament. Players have less reason to bluff in the opening rounds of the tournament because the blinds are much smaller and they can afford to wait for strong starting hands. But at the final table, it's a different story because the blinds are very high—it simply costs too much to just sit and wait for a powerful hand.

Therefore, players must try to maneuver each other out of the pot just to survive. This means that they sometimes attack each other with much weaker hands. The bottom line is that what might be a correct bluffing situation in the final stages of the tournament could get you broke in the earlier stages.

Timing is everything in executing a successful bluff. That is why getting to know your opponents is so important. Tighter players will often surrender their blinds without much of a fight. These players are easier to bluff. Loose players who frequently defend their blinds and play lots of pots are much harder to bluff. They will gamble with you. Know your man, get your hand, and then bluff!

7. DON'T GET MARRIED
TO A HAND

One of the most common mistakes that new players make is not folding a great starting hand that has been drawn out on. This usually happens when you've started with a big pair such as aces or kings, you raised before the flop, and then bet again on the flop. Then a straight card or a flush card comes on fourth street.

An opponent makes a big bet at the pot or even check-raises. You can't bear to part with your pocket rockets so you continue playing the hand when you obviously are beaten. Here's the message: You must be able to fold a great hand once in a while to preserve your precious stack of chips. It doesn't matter if your opponent started with a much weaker hand than yours—if you're beaten, you must fold.

Another great hand that often goes awry is a pocket pair to which you flopped a set. A set will win around 80 percent of the time, a very high percentage indeed. However, if your set gets drawn out on, it can become very expensive unless you have the discipline to fold your hand and avoid getting broke to it. Suppose you start with pocket sevens and the flop comes K-Q-7 with two diamonds. With a flop like that, there could be both flush and straight draws out against you.

Now the turn card comes and a 4♣ hits the board. You bet again and still get called. The river card is the J♦, making both a possible flush and a possible straight.

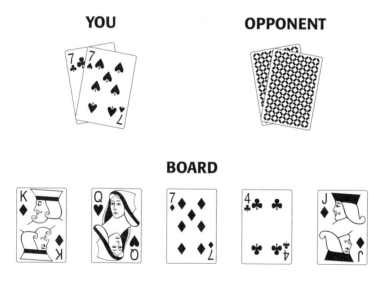

YOU　　　　　　**OPPONENT**

BOARD

An opponent, known for his tight play, moves a mountain of chips to the center of the pot. What could he have?

Judging from the way he played the hand, he almost certainly has a flush, probably the nut flush. If he made a straight, and didn't believe you were playing a flush draw since you bet twice instead of just checking to get a free card, he would probably bet a straight also. Either way you're beaten. Fold to preserve your chips.

8. RAISE MORE OFTEN THAN YOU CALL

No-limit hold'em is a bettor's game not a caller's game. Anytime you make a bet, especially a large bet, you are putting your opponent to a test. Anytime your opponent makes a big bet at you, he is putting you to a test. It is much better to be the tester than the tested.

In other words, you want to be the one who forces your opponent to guess what you have and make a decision based on speculation rather than the other way around. Most of the time he will guess wrong.

Many times you are faced with the decision to call another player's bet, fold to his bet, or raise. Of these three options, calling is usually the worst. Many times it is a choice between folding or raising—and raising is often the best option. Players frequently raise with less than premium starting hands, but when faced with a reraise from a solid player like you, they will fold.

Callers usually are losers in no-limit hold'em. Does that mean you always either raise or fold? Of course not. There are times when I suspect that my opponent may be bluffing and therefore I will simply call him down. If I'm wrong and he has a strong hand, I save money by not raising. If he is bluffing, he can't call my raise anyway, so a call is the best play.

9. PLAY GOOD TOURNAMENT STRATEGY, EVEN IN CASH GAMES

Tournament strategy is quite a bit different than cash game strategy. However, the concept of making the most money with your strong hands and losing the least money with your weaker hands is the same in both types of poker.

Think of your stack of chips as your army. The more chips you have, the greater your strength and ability to attack the enemy. The smaller your chip count, the fewer soldiers you have to fight the enemy, making you more vulnerable. Your goal is to preserve and add to your stack of chips and build your army—in both tournaments and cash games. The main difference between the two is that you can always add more chips to your stack, bring in reinforcements, between hands in a cash game, but you cannot reach into your pocket for more money during a tournament.

Playing solid poker in no-limit hold'em is the best approach to both tournaments and cash games. A wild, reckless style of play can help you get hold of a lot of chips, but keeping them is another story. Unless you tighten up your play at some point, you will eventually crash and burn.

10. SOMETIMES GIVE YOUR OPPONENTS MORE RESPECT THAN THEY DESERVE

Unless you have played with your opponents before, assume that they all know what they are doing. If this proves to be false, you can capitalize on your opponents' lack of skill later in the game. Until I see a player making what I consider to be a very bad play, I pretend that they are all great players.

You must get to know the various styles of play that your opponents use, paying special attention to the starting hands they play. Some players obviously deserve more respect than others when they enter a pot, and it is your job to be aware of who these players are and act accordingly. I also believe that being polite and respectful to your opponents is necessary. I don't like to see people get angry or upset with each other at the table, especially in casual cash games, because it often causes unnecessary tension and even forces some of your weak opponents to quit the game.

Poker is a fun game when people are laughing and having a good time. If your opponents are enjoying themselves, they are less likely to become upset when they lose their money, and will continue playing as long as they are having a good time. Paying respect to others as people as well as players is both honorable and profitable.

Now, let's move ahead a notch with a discussion of the factors that affect your success in no-limit hold'em tournaments, today's most exciting poker action.

12 POWERFUL FACTORS THAT IMPACT TOURNAMENT SUCCESS

I started playing the tournaments in 1978. When the World Series was going on, the poker games in Dallas would shut down. The same thing happened during Amarillo Slim's Super Bowl of Poker and the Stardust's Stairway to the Stars because a lot of Dallas players entered those tournaments. As the result, I became well versed in tournament play and have won the championship event in all of them except the World Series, where I placed second to Bill Smith in 1985 and Chris Ferguson fifteen years later in 2000.

Actually, anybody can win a tournament—that's the beauty of tournament poker. However, it's less likely to happen in no-limit and pot-limit hold'em than it is in other games because the skill level is so much higher. Sometimes, in a one-day tournament, a weaker player will slip through the cracks, but in the weeklong Main Event at the World Series, it's far less likely to happen. That's because no-limit hold'em is the Cadillac of poker—you can make more moves and lay more traps than in any other game. When you get down to the end in most no-limit tournaments, even the $500 buy-in ones, most of the players at the final table are recognizable. That is not the case in the limit games.

Winning one tournament doesn't make you a good player—it's winning a series of tournaments that establishes you as a *player*. All top-notch tournament players take the following factors into consideration in determining their strategy for winning.

1. CHIPS AND SITUATIONS

People used to ask me, "Why do you do well in tournaments, T.J.?" I told them that in my broke days when I was traveling two hundred miles from Shreveport to play in Dallas with just one buy-in, I got used to playing a short stack—I couldn't go to my pocket for more. In tournaments, you can't go back to your pocket, either, so I developed a style of play that protected my chips and, at the same time, built them by not taking too many chances. I soon found that the more chances you take in no-limit hold'em, the more chances you have of getting busted because you can lose all of your money in one bet. So, I learned how to survive.

Chips speak in no-limit hold'em. This is one reason why I maintain that the game doesn't really start in a no-limit tournament until the antes go into effect at the second $100/$200 level. You have to survive until you hit that point and can start taking advantage of good situations to advance.

You see, no-limit hold'em is the only game in which you can continually win pots without having a hand. You can win them with chips alone. In other games, you have to show down a hand to win, but you can win money in no-limit simply by seizing situations. Don't think that you can do this all the time or you're going to get chopped off. You have to be smart enough to pick your situations and the right time.

The thing that makes it so hard to play with just one buy-in or a short stack in no-limit hold'em ring games is that no-limit is a game designed for people who have a lot of money in front of them. To play correctly in a side game, you always want to have enough money in front of you, as much or more than any other player on the table, because that one hand might come up in which you could bust them. It's a terrible thing to have $500 while your opponent has $5,000, because if you win a pot from that man, all you can win is $500.

2. YOUR STYLE OF PLAY

In the first few rounds of a tournament, people usually try to play their best games, but over a long period of time, they're going to play their regular game. You have to be very careful and know how the player is playing at any particular time in the game. Some players come out of the shoot firing, and never change their style. They play the same from start to finish. Other players will play aggressively early and if they get some chips, then they slow down.

Hamid Dastmalchi is a great player, but early in his career I saw him go into a shell at the final table in two separate tournaments. His opponents just flat worked him over while he was in his shell and he wound up losing both times. He may have just been waiting for a big hand, or he might have been overprotecting his lead. Sometimes, players in that situation aren't playing to *win*, they're playing *not* to lose.

So, in 1992 when he won the WSOP championship, I took Hamid outside and talked to him during a break. "Look, Hamid, I'm out of the tournament," I said, "but if you're going to win it, you'd better play your style. Don't do what you did the last time. Don't shut down."

It wasn't long before a hand came up at the final table between him and Jack Keller, who'd won it in '84. Hamid raised the pot with A-K and Jack came back over the top of him. Hamid moved all in and Jack called him with almost all of his chips. Hamid won the hand with just an ace high by playing his own aggressive style.

3. OBSERVING WHILE THE CARDS ARE DEALT

I always look at my hand quickly. If you look at your hand before the action comes to you, you can see whether anything is going on behind you. If you wait until the action gets to you to look at your hand, you will miss a lot of things.

Look at your hand as soon as you get both of your cards so that you can observe the things that other players are doing when they get their cards:

- Little twitches they make when they have a hand
- Whether they slip their cards back under their chips
- Whether they are loading up, getting their chips ready to bet.

You often will be able to tell whether a player is going to play the pot. This alone will save you a lot of money because if you know that somebody behind you will either call or raise the pot, you can throw away a marginal hand that you might have called with.

4. TIMING IS CRUCIAL

Timing is everything in no-limit hold'em. It's not the hands that you play, it's *when* you play them, and who you're playing against. You might have 7-2—and I'm not telling you to play this hand—but it might be *time* to play 7-2.

A hand came up once in Dallas when I was playing against all the top players around and was running good. I was on the button looking down at one of the worst hands in hold'em, a 7-2. There were five limpers in front of me. "I'm gonna' steal this pot," I said to myself, and put in a $400 raise. Much to my dismay, three of them called me. But here came the flop:

T.J.'S HAND ON THE BUTTON

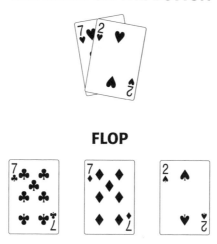

FLOP

Now, how could anybody have put me on a hand like that! Raising before the flop with this kind of hand isn't something that you want to do very often, of course. It was just a matter of timing.

Although I try to stay away from all draws in tournaments, back in 1985 a hand came up when I was playing against Bones

Berland. It was the type of year that when I played a pot, I won it. I was on the button with the 6♥ 3♥.

There were two or three limpers in front of me who were somewhat weak. I thought that I'd just pick up the pot right then and win enough antes for a few free rounds. I was sitting there with about $40,000 in chips and raised the pot $1,000. Bones called me. The flop came:

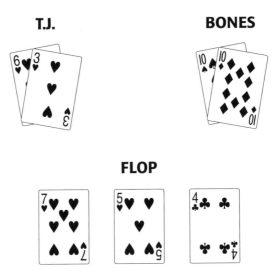

T.J.   **BONES**

FLOP

Bones made a bet at the pot and I raised him. He called for all of his money with his pocket tens. Of course, I busted him, but it was just a matter of timing. If Bones had come in with a raise, I would have had to muck my hand, but he didn't, and I was able to play off of his mistake.

Of course, nobody is good enough to be mistake free—but those who make fewer mistakes will win the money. This is why you have to continue to learn all the time you're playing. I've been playing for a lot of years, and I learn something new every day about how other players play a hand.

5. POKER IS A GAME OF MISTAKES

What does poker break down to in the long run? Most of the money you make comes from somebody's mistakes. You cannot win in a poker game if everybody in the game plays perfectly. If the cards break even in a no-limit poker game, Tom and I figure to win. Any player figures to win if his skill level is superior to his opponents.

Good players also make mistakes, but they make fewer of them. A good player doesn't hope to get a 60-40 break in the cards. If the cards break even, a good player will win the money at all times because he's going to make fewer mistakes than a bad player will make.

Here's a story about a simple mistake that was made in a small no-limit hold'em hold'em tournament at Crystal Park in California. Tom was in the big blind with the 6♠ 3♠ against the chip leader, who had been playing every hand. Now, you wouldn't think that you could make a mistake by folding a 6-3, right? But folding in this situation was a mistake.

He had one-half of his chips in the pot, and would have to put in two of his three remaining chips on the very next hand. The circumstances made it a mistake to fold the 6-3, not because it figured to be the best starting hand, but because he already had half of his money in the pot and should have played the two suited cards. If he didn't figure the raiser to be holding a pair, the worst off he could have been was a 2 to 1 underdog. Unfortunately, he lost the next hand and was out of the tournament.

One of the biggest mistakes that people make in no-limit hold'em is raising the pot with a medium pair from early position, leaving themselves open to a reraise. If a good player knows that Player A is the type of player that raises with these types of hands, sooner or later he's going to pop him with nothing and make Player A lay down his hand. If you call the raise with a medium pair from up front, then you're compounding your mistake. Ninety-nine percent of the time, you should just throw that medium pair away because it simply cannot stand a reraise.

You have to be very selective about the hands that you raise with. For example, an A-K or A-Q is a very sensible hand to raise with from around back, but it's not a good hand to raise with from up front, especially if someone pops you. The A-K is called "Walking Back to Houston" because so many old-time road gamblers got broke with the hand, even lost their cars betting with it, and (figuratively speaking) had to "walk" over two hundred miles back to Houston from Dallas.

Another mistake players make is trying to chop off a guy because he's getting way out of line. If you think that way, you can get caught in the middle, especially when you're playing in a full game. Shoot at one player when you're only playing one player. Otherwise, don't set your sights on one opponent in the game. Don't make the mistake of saying to yourself, "Well, I'm a better player than this guy, and he's going to make a mistake, and I'm just going to gobble him up." Invariably, you will be caught in the middle and somebody behind you will knock you off.

6. BUILDING AND PROTECTING YOUR CHIPS

In tournaments, you have to build your chips, but you also have to protect your chips. Therefore, you have to be very, very careful, especially in the early rounds while the tables are still full. Suppose that you have the $1,000 that you started with and you look around and see one player with $5,000, another one with $8,000. That should not affect your play one iota. You can't control *their* stacks, you can only control *your own* stack.

Having chips early in the tournament doesn't necessarily mean anything. The big stack's rush may be over by the time it gets down to the nitty-gritty, something that happens most of the time. Many times, the early chip leaders are not *good* players—they're *lucky* players who have been playing a lot of pots. Even though they have the chip lead, they will make enough mistakes in the later stages that their stacks will dwindle because they continue to play too many hands.

You have to be selective in the hands that you play in no-limit hold'em. In tournaments, the one overriding factor that you always have to consider is, "I must survive to have a chance to win." You have to think about that all of the time. This is why I play a conservative game early. I don't worry about how many chips I have early in the tournament; I'm a plodder. I know that the opportunities will come. My ultimate scenario is that at the end of every break, I have more chips than I had at the previous break.

In the late rounds, protecting your chips is also important. I remember the story of a player who got to the final table in second chip position. She was holding an ace-rag in 10-handed play when she decided to make a play at the only person at the table who could have busted her, a guy who had been playing every hand. The flop came with two face cards and she bluffed off all of her money against the other big stack, who called her bluff with second pair.

Who made the bigger mistake—the guy who had been playing every hand, or the one who decided to go after him in a full ring? She was more out of line because she had chips to protect. Also, she didn't raise him enough to prevent him from calling. When she raised, she should have showered down on him with the raise.

Another mistake that was made in the play of this hand was going up against another big stack. When you're in this type of situation, you want to attack the small stacks and stay clear of the other big stacks when you don't hold the nuts, because they are the ones that can really hurt you. You want to play against the big stacks when you have a premium hand because you want to double through them; but with less than a premium hand, you don't want to mess with them.

7. THE TOURNAMENT STRUCTURE

The difference between pot-limit and no-limit tournaments is that in no-limit, an ante goes in when you hit the second level of the $100/$200 blinds. That is, during the first level of $100/$200 blinds, there is no ante; but when it goes to the second level of $100/$200 blinds (usually about the fourth or fifth round of play), the ante goes into effect, beginning at $25. This is the way it's done at the World Series of Poker and at all other major tournaments.

In pot-limit, there is never an ante, so it is always cheaper to play a hand in a pot-limit tournament than it is to play a hand in no-limit. When you get up into the $100/$200 blinds in no-limit, you're also anteing $25 a hand, so it's costing you $525 a round to play. But I have always maintained that the *main* difference between pot-limit and no-limit tournament play is that you can play weaker hands in pot-limit than you can in no-limit.

8. THE LUCK FACTOR

Kenny Flaton was the last one with a chance to win the car at the Bicycle Club's tournament in 1996. If he won the tournament, he would win the all-around best player award as well as the car, so he wasn't giving one dime away. Kenny brought in the pot for a decent raise and Paul Ladanyi reraised him. Kenny went over the top for all of his chips with the "two eyes of Texas," pocket aces, just what he was supposed to have. Paul had the 7♥ 4♥ in his hand. For no reason that I could see, Paul put in all of his chips, ended up making three sevens, and busted Kenny out of the tournament at a time when Paul himself could have been knocked out by the play.

Later in the tournament, Paul moved all in with a Q-9 over a raise by another player who had A-K, and won the pot. Another situation came up between Paul and me when I had two nines. I raised the pot three-handed with the nines and he moved all in over the top of me holding a Q-10. I called him. At least he had two overcards in this situation, but there is no way that he could have known this. The flop came K-Q-10, giving him queens and tens. But on fourth street came a jack, giving me a straight. Then on fifth street came another 10, giving him a full house. I hadn't hesitated to call him because I had observed all of the other hands that he had played.

I had all of this in the back of my mind during the first no-limit tournament at the Commerce Club's L. A. Poker Championship in 1997. Paul raised on the button three or four times, and I came back over the top of him three or four times to take the pot away from him. Most of those times, I had a hand but a few times, I didn't. I said to myself, "Now I'm setting this man up; he's going to make a play at me." In no-limit, you can set up plays and opponents by your previous plays. That's why I'll show a hand once in a while when I have bluffed: I want someone to see my hand. I play it like a finely coiled cobra just waiting for somebody to open the lid on the basket.

Sure enough, a hand came down in which Paul brought it in and I made a small raise. He said, "All in!" I had $42,000 at the time and he had $24,000. All I had was A-J offsuit, but in my mind, there was no doubt that I had the best hand, so I called him. You have to show your hand when you're all-in at the final table in a tournament. He turned over a 9-6 offsuit.

My play was exactly right. My timing was right. I had set him up. I was a 2 to 1 favorite, and that's big enough to get in all of your money before the flop. The flop came 9-9-8. Paul wound up winning the hand and the tournament.

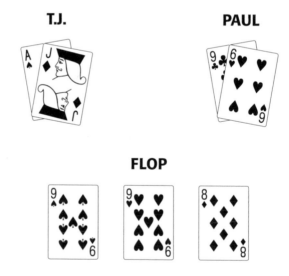

T.J.   **PAUL**

FLOP

This is just another example that illustrates how the luck factor comes into play in poker. You can set up all the plays in the world, you can play perfectly on a hand, and you can still lose. And there's nothing that you can do about it.

9. THE CLOCK

At the start of a new round, players who have been playing in an ultra-conservative fashion sometimes start going to the center with what appears to be reckless abandon, especially in no-limit tournaments. For people who have been watching all of the prior conservative action from the rail, it seems like a bell has gone off and people are now racing to the center with all of their chips.

A good example of this occurs when there is a sharp jump in the blinds and antes of a major tournament. For example some tournaments jump from a $25 ante, $100/$200 blind structure to a $50 ante, $200/$400 blind structure. You know that you can't just sit around and wait for big hands because the blind and ante increases will eat you up. Therefore, you must open up your game and take more risks. Sometimes this big jump does not occur until Day Two of a big-field tournament.

Conservative play usually is correct and is the norm for Day One because the blinds are still relatively small, but with this emphasis on faster play during Day Two, a similar approach will not get the money. You can hang on for a long time on Day One playing regular ring-game strategy, but the time factor clicks in on Day Two. The carnage during those first two hours of Day Two is quite extensive. By the end of Day One of slow-action tournaments with two-hour rounds, approximately 45 percent of the field has been eliminated. After the *first round* of Day Two, the field usually gets pared down to fewer than one-third of the original entrants.

When the increases in blinds and antes are more gradual, the clock is less of a factor in your game strategy. But when the increases begin to double at the beginning of each new round, the clock becomes far more important. At that point, you can't just sit there and hope that a conservative approach will come through for you. This is true of all major tournaments. Any time the tournament gets to about the fourth or fifth level of play when the blinds and antes double at every round, you can't just sit there any longer playing conservatively and hope to be successful: You have to reevaluate your strategy.

Of course, the larger your stack, the less concern you have for the clock at any level. I am more concerned about the clock when I have a short stack because I know that the blinds and antes can eat me alive. And if I'm quite a way into the tournament (when the blinds and antes are doubling up every round), I know that I'm going to be playing short-handed pretty soon because a lot of players will be dropping out.

I have won a lot of the last hands at the end of a level. I know that people are itching to get up and take a break, so the last few hands in the round are sometimes good places to pick up a pot here and there.

10. MATH AND POKER

The math of poker should be in the back of your mind all the time. For most of the top pros, it is automatic. They can make their decisions quickly because they understand the numbers. But when you watch some players, you can practically see the numbers clicking in their eyes like a mental calculator. You can tell that they are methodically figuring out things such as:

- Is the pot laying me enough odds to make such and such a play?
- What are my chances?
- What's the math behind my hand?

That type of intense deliberation can be a big tell on somebody, a huge tell in fact, because you know they have a hand that they're trying to compute. The hand isn't strong enough for them to know immediately whether to play it. It's a "decision" hand that they're trying to figure out whether to play based on pot odds and other factors.

In tournament poker, pot odds aren't always the most important factor in deciding whether to play a hand. It goes out the window a lot of times because you can't go back to your pocket for more chips—and that should be a determining factor in each and every hand. You should take the math into consideration, yes, but if that's all you're thinking about—and you forget about the fact that if you don't win the pot, you will either be out of the tournament or you will take a big hit to your stack—you are putting too much importance on it. Your thinking in critical tournament situations has to be different from your thinking in a cash game.

You should know what you're going to do with any card that comes out before that card is dealt. That way, most of the time, you will be able to act fast on your hand and not give away any information. Very few times do I take any time at all on a hand because I'm aware of which cards will help me and which ones won't help me. And I know what I'm going to do if those cards show up. In other words, when I go into a hand, I have already planned what my play is going to be after the flop, depending on the number of players in the hand.

11. THE NATURE OF NO-LIMIT POTS

Most of the pots that you will play in no-limit hold'em tournaments are going to be two-way hands, except in the early stages when there might be some four and five-way hands. A lot of players limp early in the tournament. Although some of them are limping in with drawing hands, my whole idea is to let *them* play the drawing hands, not me. I'm trying *not* to play them.

I got knocked out of the WSOP one time on a drawing hand. I was in the big blind with A♥ 5♥. Gabe Kaplan had brought it in from the first seat for $200 during the second level of play. There were five callers when it got around to me, so I threw in $150 to make the call. The flop came A-3-4, with the 3♥ 4♥. I had top pair, a straight draw, and a straight flush draw. I checked from the blind, Gabe made a big bet at the pot, and I moved all in on him with a check-raise.

T.J.   **GABE**

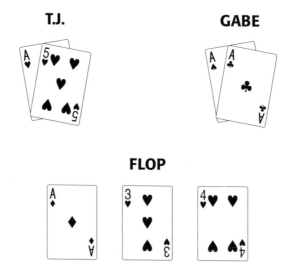

FLOP

He had the other two aces in the hole, and I missed all my draws. In this situation, if I hadn't put in the $150 to start with—get me right, when I *knew* I didn't have the best hand— I would have still been in the tournament instead of getting broke on the hand. In that instance, I was thinking, "Well, I've got pot odds," and that's what made me play it.

Many times in this situation, I would have won that pot with the check-raise. When I got called, I knew I had the worst hand at the moment, but with so many outs, I still had a chance of winning it. I played my hand on the flop the way it should have been played, but the big question came up *before* the flop.

When you have a questionable calling hand, you have to ask yourself, "What am I hoping to flop?" There have been many times in ring games when I have called with a hand like 6♥ 5♥ in a raised pot from around back with four or five players already in the pot. I'd hate to tell you how often I've flopped a straight and a flush draw with a hand like that—and never made a dime with it.

When you get the big flop, what are you trying to make? Say the flop comes 3-4-8 with two hearts when you're holding the 6♥ 5♥.

YOU

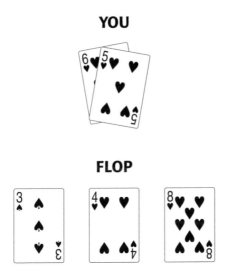

FLOP

Now you're going to play the hand, and probably play it strongly. But if you hadn't played the 6-5 to begin with, you wouldn't have been in any trouble. What you really have is just a 6-high hand.

12. PLAYING A PATIENT, MISTAKE-FREE GAME

People have a tendency to get nervous during a tournament. When they do, they start making mistakes. To repeat, no-limit hold'em is a game of mistakes. If other players aren't making mistakes, you aren't going to win. If *you* aren't making mistakes, *they* aren't going to win.

All top players not only make fewer mistakes, they capitalize on other people's mistakes. If you don't play perfect poker (or don't get extremely lucky) against top players, they will beat you. Period. None of the top players think of themselves as being lucky—if anything, they think of themselves as being unlucky. But all of them are patient in waiting for the right cards, the right situation, the right time to make a play. In fact, no-limit hold'em probably is the most patient of all the poker games.

However, if you're too patient—if you wait so long for a playable hand that your chips start growing cobwebs—you aren't going to get there very often because you're playing too tight. Your play becomes too predictable. You have to be very flexible as situations arise while you are going through the stages of a tournament. This is why some otherwise good poker players who do well in cash games do not fare well in tournaments. You cannot play the same style all the time in a tournament, you must adapt to the ebb and flow of the competition.

In the next chapter, we detail specific strategies and tactics that will take you to the top of the tournament ladder.

4 PLAYING TO WIN BEFORE THE FLOP

You must be very careful about the quality of your starting hands if you hope to survive long enough to have a shot at winning the tournament. In the first round of the Main Event at the World Series of Poker, as well as in the first round of the smaller buy-in events at the WSOP, even a pair of kings is not a big enough hand to get broke with before the flop. The only hand that big is two aces.

TYPES OF HANDS TO START WITH IN EARLY POSITION

In the early positions, you only want to play A-K or better. When I say A-K or better, I'm not talking about playing the small pairs, although you might limp with a pair of eights or better. If I am holding A-Q (suited or unsuited) *or worse* in the first four or five seats, I don't want to put even a dime in the pot during the first few levels in a full nine- or ten-handed game.

Always treat being suited as a little added luxury, a factor that should not change your decision to play a hand that you ordinarily would not play. Your hand is still A-Q—being suited is just an added bonus. The value of the hand is in its ranks, not in its being suited. You cannot stand a good raise with the A-Q from an early position in the opening rounds. If you catch either the ace or the queen, you are put into a quandary about what to do next if someone bets at you. Do you throw it away, do you raise, or do you call? Why put yourself in that situation?

Try to avoid having to make any tricky decisions. You would rather come in with any pair than an A-Q in those first four spots because a small-to-medium pair plays very easily after the flop. It's simple: No set, no bet. Playing A-Q or A-J, however, requires a lot of finesse and judgment after the flop if you get any action. Don't misunderstand, however: We do not recommend playing small pairs from up front.

THE RAISING HANDS
FROM EARLY POSITION

For the percentage of times that you raise before the flop, you are reraised very few times in no-limit hold'em. In the first four positions, the raising hands are big pairs—queens or better, *not* jacks or better—and A-K, if you feel good about the hand. Nothing is wrong with making a small raise with A-K, but a lot of players who have moved up from limit hold'em to no-limit tournaments will move in with a big number of chips when they hold A-K. Why put all those chips in jeopardy when you don't have anything yet? Just make a standard raise.

For example, if you're still in the first round with $25/$50 blinds, bring it in for $200 or $300. I've seen novice players bring in the A-K for $4,000 or $5,000 with everybody sitting behind them. What if somebody wakes up with aces or kings? In a situation where you have overbet the pot, you're not going to get action unless you're beaten. You're either going to win $75 (the blinds) or lose a ton of chips. That's one either-or situation you can avoid by making an appropriate bet.

THE STARTING HANDS IN MIDDLE POSITION

You can lower your standards a little when you are in middle position—seats five, six, and seven in nine-handed play. You can play a hand such as A-10 *suited* or above if all of the players in front of you have passed.

The A-10 is one hand that I recommend playing suited. If I were going to play a big ace (A-10 on up), the hand would need to be suited because of that slight edge that it offers in possibly flopping a flush. You still have players behind you, so you have to be able to stand a raise. You should always ask yourself, "If I play this hand and get raised, can I play it?" Of course, *who* raises you also affects your decision.

You need to be watching how the flow of the game is going, what kinds of cards your opponents are playing. Are they the types who would be likely to raise you with a K-Q or K-J, or maybe a baby ace (an ace with a small kicker)? You have to be observant enough to know those answers. When you bring it in without raising with a hand like A-10 or above from a middle position, you're just hoping to catch a flop.

THE DANGER HANDS

If there is any raising before the flop, hands such as K-J, Q-10, and K-Q can be dangerous to play. You will get in far less trouble playing a 9-8 than you will a Q-J, because it is easier to get away from the middle drawing hand. An A-10 and A-J also can be dangerous, because players often will slip into an unraised pot with A-K or A-Q.

The question is, "What do you have if you flop something to one of these hands?"

Of course, it is far better to flop your second pair than your top pair, if your second rank card is the highest card on the flop; but even then you could be in trouble. For example, if you play the Q-J and flop jacks, you are in kicker trouble.

These types of hands require the most careful decisions and the most skill. I might play these kinds of hands if I can open the pot with them—if I'm on the button in an unopened pot, for example—but I don't play them if I can only call with them, even from a late position. Say that you have K-J and it is passed to you on the button. Then you might play this hand. It depends on who is left in the pot: The more timid the players, the more likely I will be to raise, but the more aggressive the players, the more likely I will be to just flat call. Some aggressive players don't respect any type of raise, and although they may figure that you have a better hand than they have, they're not going to give it up, and they may be able to outflop you.

In a no-limit tournament, I won't even venture into the pot from the first five positions with A-Q if it's early in the tournament. It's different when you're playing short-handed. But early in the tournament with a full table, I won't play an A-Q. Again, if somebody raises, what do you do with this hand?

THE RAISING HANDS AND THE RERAISING HANDS

Referring back to our earlier discussions, you know by now which players will bring it in for raises with smaller pairs. Unless you have an opponent pigeonholed as a player who often raises with small pairs, the only two hands that you can reraise the pot with are kings and aces. Queens definitely are out of the question, unless you're against the small-pair raiser, or unless you're sitting in a favorable position.

Suppose the player in the number-one seat brings it in for a raise and you're sitting in third position with two queens. If you reraise from this spot, you still have six players sitting behind you who could have aces or kings and might re-pop you, in which case you could get into a lot of trouble with your queens.

There is nothing wrong with flat calling with two queens or two jacks. You can save your reraises for when the table is down to three or four-handed. With the medium large pairs—tens, jacks, or queens—you might want to reraise short-handed, but you would never reraise with them in a full ring.

Although aces and kings are the only two hands that you can reraise with, there are two ways of playing them. I often play "second-hand low" and take a chance on them. In second-hand low, somebody brings it in for a raise when you have kings or aces in a position that is very close to the original bettor, who is sitting up front. You flat call and hope that somebody behind you will reraise the pot and drive him back into you so that you can put it to him before the flop.

The other approach that I might take is to make a minimal raise that I know won't hurt my stack. Then, if I don't flop to them, I can get rid of them.

POCKET ACES: RAISE OR LIMP?

Cardinal rule number one in no-limit hold'em is this: If you limp with aces, you will never get broke with aces.

RAISE OR LIMP?

The reason that you limp with aces before the flop is so that someone behind you will raise and give you the opportunity to reraise. If you flat call with them before the flop and nobody raises, four or five players may limp into the pot behind you with all sorts of random hands. The more people in the pot, the more chance you're going to get beaten. So, if one of them comes out swinging on the flop, you can simply throw your aces away and you haven't lost anything except your original bet. Nobody has seen your hand; nobody knows that you have limped with aces, so just throw them away.

If you're in a later stage of a tournament where you have a shorter stack than your opponents, you would be making a mistake if you limp with aces. In this scenario, you have to raise with them because you don't have a lot of chips, and it means something to you when you play a pot.

But if you have a lot of chips and decide to limp with aces, you haven't really lost anything except your original bet if you lose with them. You want to *protect* your big stack, and try to *build* your short stack. With a big stack, you also could raise a pretty big amount to start with if you want to gamble.

Just remember the rule: If you limp with aces, you never get broke with aces. Two aces are the best starting hand you can get, but when two small pair are out there, all you have is one pair of aces, Eke and Ike, American Airlines.

RAISING BEFORE THE FLOP

There are three reasons to raise in no-limit hold'em:

(1) To get more money in the pot (get a call)
(2) To isolate, or
(3) To try to win the pot right there.

If four limpers are in the pot and you have a big pair, you want to reduce the number of players to one or two, so you make a big enough raise to guarantee it. You don't want the limpers to flop two rag pairs, for example, and beat your big pair, so you try to get them out before the flop.

No-limit is a game in which you never actually have to build a pot. When you move in on them, there are a lot of players who will call a raise for all of their chips with a hand like A-Q. They're not good players, but they are out there.

Usually, when you are the first one in the pot and decide to bring it in for a raise, you can raise three to five times the size of the big blind. If someone already has trailed in, you might scale the raise upward a notch or so.

HOW MUCH WILL THEY CALL?

When you want a call, one way to get it is to make a raise that is the size that you think your opponents will call. Some players will stand a bigger raise than others when they decide to play a hand, so you raise an amount that you think they will pay to see the next card. Player A might be the type who will call you for $300; Player B might call if you raise as much as $600. These are the types of things that you learn from observation.

Players who are new to no-limit play often ask whether they should base the size of their raise on the amount of chips they have in front of them. No, the only time that you use a percentage of your chips to determine how much you raise is when you're at the final table with, say, five players left.

Suppose two tables are left with five players at each table. You're playing down to the final nine players who will go to the last table. You pick up a hand such as 10-10, J-J, or Q-Q and you decide to raise the pot.

Now you have to make a decision: If you raise the pot, are you willing to play for all of your chips? In this case, I would raise with at least one-half of my chips, if I didn't put them all in to begin with, to try to shut them all out. Or, you might want somebody to play with a lesser pair. If somebody makes a play back at you, you are pot committed.

You have made sure that you're mentally committed to this pot. And then you simply go with it.

Frequently, I see players bring in two queens or two jacks for $400 or so, somebody reraises, and they throw away their big pairs. About a quarter of the time, you will lay down the best hand, because you're playing smart poker. But when you are playing five-handed or less in a poker tournament and you're getting short on chips, you want to commit yourself to the pot when you bring it in for a raise. When you raise with one-half or more of your chips, you know that you're going to go for the rest of them if you have to.

SETTING THE STANDARD

The player who makes the first big raise at the table usually sets the standard at each level. Say that we're anteing a quarter ($25) and the blinds are $100/$200, making $525 in the pot to start with. If I were going to raise, I would make it $700; in other words, a little bit more than the total money in the pot. Usually, in cases like this, for whatever the amount of my first raise, the other players will follow that standard.

VARYING THE SIZE OF YOUR BETS

Since you're playing no-limit, you can vary the size of your bets according to the players you're up against, whereas in pot-limit, your raises must be a standard size. This is one reason why no-limit hold'em is a much better game for top players. Pot-limit has more skill to it than limit poker, but no-limit has far more skill than pot-limit. The real art in pot-limit is in building a pot, but in no-limit, you don't have to do that. Your goal is to extricate as much money from your opponents as you can, and there are a lot of ways of doing that.

All of your chips can be in jeopardy in no-limit at any time—before the flop, on the flop, on fourth street, and on fifth street. When people flop big hands in no-limit hold'em, there often is no action until fifth street, and then there may be a lot of it.

Some players will move their raises around, bet $600 one time, $1,500 the next, $1,000 on another hand. They are unintentionally giving out information by varying the size of their raise. So, I suggest that you always raise by about the same amount, an amount that is commensurate with the level that you are playing. In this way, people cannot use the amount of your raise to pigeonhole you on a hand.

Some people have used three-to-four times the size of the big blind to gauge the size of their raises, but I don't use that method. I gauge my bets more by the size of the pot. Say that you're anteing $100 and the blinds are $300/$600. At that level, it is costing you $1,800 in antes and blinds every nine hands to play the round. You can pick up more pots as the limits get higher; in fact, you have to pick them up just to stay alive. And so, I probably would bring it in for $2,000 at the $300/$600 level, just a little bit more than what is in the pot. That's enough to make players stop and think, "Do I want to risk $2,000 to play this hand? Am I willing to sacrifice $2,000 to possibly win $4,000?"

One top player that I know who does well in these situations will move in all of his chips when he's sitting in late position. He doesn't do it from the front, just from around the back. He might have two sixes in his hand with $25,000 sitting in front of him, and move his entire stack in from, say, sixth or seventh position because he is the first to act. He will even do it with A-6. He makes a monster opening raise to pick up the blinds. He thinks that he has the best hand, and he is afraid to get played with—he just wants to win the blinds. I'm not sure I agree with that strategy: To sacrifice $25,000 to win $4,000 doesn't make much sense to me.

The thought that I always keep in my mind is that if the first four players don't have anything, there is a chance that the last five players *do* have something. So, if you're in middle to late position and the action is passed to you, why would you put in all of your money? Unless, of course, you do it as a flat bluff.

THE NO-POSITION BLINDS IN NO-LIMIT HOLD'EM

The number one fact to remember about the blinds is this: You have position before the flop, but you're in the worst position at the table after the flop.

When we talk about position at the table in a 10-handed game in the boot camps I teach, here's how we put it: The first two or three seats after the big blind are early position. The next two or three seats are middle position. The cutoff seat and the button are late position. The blinds are "no position." That's right—we don't even consider them to be a position.

It takes a stronger hand to play out of the little blind than the big blind. If you get a free ride in the big blind, it really is free. But the small blind always costs something to see the flop. That's why I don't believe in doing something like this: You have Q-3 in the small blind and everybody limps in for the minimum, so you put the other half a bet to see the flop. I know for a fact that Q-3 or any two random cards may hit once in a while, but they may not hit for a week either. Do this every time and see how much money it costs you.

People make a common mistake from the big blind when they call a raise without a premium hand. For example, suppose you're in the big blind in a $5/$10 game, and somebody makes it $30 to go. You have J-8 suited and say to yourself, "Well, hell, it's only $20 more."

Say that 10 times and it's $200 more! You're always taking much the worst of it from the blinds.

You might be able to play some hands in middle or late position that you cannot play in early position—but if you cannot play a hand in early position, you sure as hell can't play it in the blinds. Of course that's not cut and dried, because there are a few hands you can play from the blinds, but only because you have some money in the pot. For example, say that you have A-J in first position. You throw the hand away, of course. But if a few players have limped into the pot and it will only cost you one-half a bet in the small blind, then sure, you'll play your A-J. You might even play the little pairs for half a bet in that situation.

But what do you do if it's raised when you're in the blinds with these kinds of hands? Now you have a tricky decision to make. Suppose you have 3-3 in the little blind. The pot was raised early and a couple of players called. Are you going to call the raise from the little blind? You might. But what if one player raised from early position and nobody called. Now, are you going to play it from the small blind? No, of course not, because you realize that even if all the raiser has is a 5-4, he's only an 11 to 10 underdog to you. This is where discipline and position come to the forefront in making good decisions.

PLAYING THE BLINDS IN TOURNAMENTS

Tom will often protect his blind in tournament play. He tells a story about a time when he got broke in the big blind making a judgment call. "I was in the big blind in a no-limit tournament at the Queens Classic with A-9 offsuit and Thomas Chung was in the small blind. The action was passed to Brent Carter, who raised on the button. Carter didn't have to have a hand to raise; he had been playing a lot of pots and had a big pile of chips in front of him. With only a fraction of the bet in front of him, Chung called all-in from the small blind.

"I knew that Chung was ready to make a stand with anything, so I thought that I had a reasonable chance of having the best hand in this situation. I overcalled for all of my chips, making the side pot far larger than the main pot. Carter was holding J-9 offsuit and spiked a jack on fourth street to beat me. Chung took the main pot with pocket aces."

Dana Smith had been sweating Tom during the tournament. She remarked that since Tom was low on chips and had enough to meet the small blind with some chips left over, he could have mucked the hand and then waited for the button. While that's true, Tom's decision in this case was spot on. He was playing the players and knew that Carter, with a ton of chips in front of him, didn't necessarily have to be holding a hand to make the raise. Also, if Chung had had enough chips to call the full raise, Tom would have thrown the hand away, because he would have been more afraid of Chung's call than of Carter's raise. The only way that you can avoid these types of situations is by never making those kinds of calls—yet it is exactly this kind of call that separates the men from the boys in no-limit hold'em.

Here is another example from tournament play. A man raised in the small blind and I was in the big blind with A-K. He made a decent raise, but I moved in on him. He did not hesitate to call me. He went into the pot with a 6-3 offsuit and won the pot with a pair of sixes. When the hand was all over, he said, "I knew you didn't have anything." That was the most ridiculous statement I have ever heard in my life—he knew that *I* didn't have anything, but *he* had a 6 high! I didn't mind losing the pot as much as I did hearing that statement.

PICKING UP THE BLINDS

The blinds are vulnerable positions, and you can pick up a lot of them late in a tournament, especially from the button. If you don't have at least a semi-good hand in the blind, you have no business calling bets with it.

Say that someone raises the blind, and you have a J-8 or something similar. You might think to yourself, "Well, he's just trying to pick up my blind, so maybe I'll call him and hit the flop and pick him off." Ninety percent of the time, you'll be taking the worst of it. It's tough not to defend the blinds, especially if a very aggressive player is on the button, but you have to give up those types of hands.

In a different scenario, suppose you have a K-Q in the big blind in a short-handed game, an aggressive player raises from the button, and the little blind folds. Now, you might have a shot. In this case, I might even reraise. At other times, the button might be raising with A-rag and have me beaten. You have to make a decision in these situations.

DEFENDING THE BLIND

There is nothing wrong with defending your blind with K-J or K-Q against a guy who always raises on the button in a short-handed game. But a lot of players will always defend their blinds against a small raise if the blinds are a decent size. If an aggressive player like Phil Hellmuth thinks that nobody will play back at him from the blinds, he will attack every time. But I will play back at these types of players, sometimes without a hand, and force them to be more careful about raising my blind. They don't know when I'm going to do it—and neither do I!

I might let them take my blind two or three times and then come back over the top of them. This play does two things: It scares the pants off of them, and because the pot has been raised, you have all the money back that they have stolen from you in the other pots. You can lose three steals in a row, and then on their fourth steal attempt, you can regain your money plus a little. When you try this steal-back, you want to make a big enough raise so that you can win the pot without seeing a flop. The message that you're sending them is, "My blind is not yours all of the time."

There also are players who will defend their blinds against aggressive button players because they get sick and tired of being run over, or their pride gets insulted. You don't want to let your ego play your hand. If you're in the blind with an aggressive player who often raises on the button, you need to be very careful about what you call the raise with. Set your standards pretty high, especially in a full ring.

BLUFFING BEFORE THE FLOP

People's perception of bluffing in no-limit hold'em is somewhat erroneous. Watching a bluff pan out on television is exciting, but in reality, players bluff far less often in no-limit hold'em than most people think.

Before the flop, the bluff positions are the button and the little blind. Players bluff more often from those positions than from any other spot. Although I can't say that I never bluff from the button or the small blind, most of the time I try to use a reverse from those positions—I want to be in a bluff position *with* a hand so that my opponents will think that I am bluffing, and someone with a weaker hand will call me. But unless you can show them a hand, you can't bluff from any position—you must be able to show them a hand when you are called.

I bluff as much or more than most people, but I like to bluff from a different position than the so-called standard ones. For example, I like to bluff from the first seat; I've done it lots of times. When you come in for a raise under the gun, that's a strength position. You don't want to put in all of your chips, just a good-sized raise. You usually try a front position bluff or semibluff when you just need to pick up a pot. It's a far stronger bluff because your opponents are going to give you credit for a hand since you raised from the front. Of course, it's far riskier than bluffing from the back.

If an unknown player, or one that you don't consider to be a top player (and who isn't a maniac), puts in a front position raise, you usually can give him more credit for having a hand that you can give to someone like me or Tom. If a player like that raises from the front, I can guarantee you that I will throw my hand away unless I have kings or aces. A player like Poker Hall of Famer Barbara Enright, who understands position, might put in a bluff or semibluff raise from the first seat in a short-handed game, but she will never do it without a hand in a full ring. She can be an absolute machine gunner, but she also can settle down when she needs to and play very solid poker.

All of the big pots usually are hand against hand, big bluff against big bluff. To use an old Southern poker expression, it's the old "iron balls" theory: Most of the top players have guts. They are not afraid to put a man on a certain hand and then sacrifice all of their chips on a bluff. It's really a grandstand play and, with me, it happens at least once in a tournament.

Say that you have put in a raise and your opponent comes over the top of you for a decent reraise. You have him on a hand, but not aces or kings. So, you show some guts and come back over the top of him to try to make him lay down his hand. This type of move happens, but you have to be willing to take a big risk. When you're talking about bluffing, that is the ultimate bluff.

You're not likely to take that much of a chance early in the tournament, but at some time during the event, a situation will come up when you can do it. And even though you totally know your man, and you absolutely know that the situation is right, you're still taking a chance because anybody can pick up two aces or two kings and bust you.

It all depends on the "feel" factor, your timing. I don't care if you wrote fifty books about poker, you still couldn't teach a person that little thing that you are born with. "Feel" gives the top players an edge over the next-to-the-top players. It separates the men from the boys, not in the sense of gender, but in the sense of being superior versus being very good at poker.

I can't count how many tournaments I've survived without holding any cards, by strategically picking up a pot here and there to stay alive. But let me say it again: If you cannot show winning hands, you cannot bluff in poker. If players see that you're not catching anything, you sure as hell can't bluff them. The only way that you can bluff in pot-limit and no-limit poker is if you're able to show a bunch of hands, because then the other players will give you credit for a hand.

You may be wondering why we haven't discussed playing Big Slick, small pairs and small connectors in this chapter. That's because we think it's so important to play them correctly, we've devoted an entire chapter to playing Big Slick and another full chapter to playing little pairs and connectors. Now let's move right along to strategies for playing after the flop.

5 PLAYING TO WIN AFTER THE FLOP

Whereas a lot of amateurs would rather win the pot before the flop, most professional players want to play flops because they believe they can outplay you after the flop. And, of course, they figure to win more money that way. Here are a few tips to help you compete with skill and confidence from the flop to the river.

BIG PAIRS AFTER THE FLOP

Aces, kings, and queens are *big* pairs. If you have raised before the flop with A-A, K-K or Q-Q, and no overcards come on the flop, it is correct to make a bet in no-limit hold'em. But keep in mind that all you have is an overpair. You have to know the players that you are playing with so that if somebody comes back over the top of you, you can decide what to do with your hand. Are you going to call or fold?

If you lead bet and get raised on the flop, you must decide whether you're going to go through with your pair or throw it away. Assuming that no draws are possible on the board, there is a pretty good chance that your opponent has either a set or two pair, or he may have called your raise with some crazy hand. Suppose you have pocket kings and the flop comes Q-J-7.

YOU

FLOP

Your first worry is that your opponent has flopped a set, although he could also have queens and jacks for two pair. If he's a weak player, he could have any two pair.

Remember that some weak players call raises with any two connectors or suited cards. If someone has raised in front of you before the flop and that player leads at the pot on the flop, you definitely don't try to shut him out right then. You smooth call him. If you are the one who leads on the flop and an opponent who is a *player* smooth calls your bet, an alarm should go off in your head: "Boy, I'd better shut down now."

Ask yourself why he has called you.

More mistakes are made in these types of situations than almost anywhere else. A player will go through with the hand and then a deuce comes on fourth street, for example. Thinking that his opponent might have a drawing hand such as a K-10, the lead bettor makes a big bet at the pot to try to shut him out. If you make that kind of bet and your opponent comes over the top of you, you're a gone goose.

Always remember that all of your chips are in jeopardy on any one hand, so play smart. Know when to give credit, and when to shut down. These judgments all come from knowing your opponents. Everything in this book evolves from the first chapter on knowing how your opponents play in different situations. If you've been in a tournament for three or four hours, you've already seen a lot of situations come up that give you information about how your opponents play.

In the chapter titled "Tournament Action Hands," we give you more examples of tournament action hands when you have A-A, K-K and Q-Q.

When You Flop a Set

Now suppose that you flop your set. Whether it is top set or middle set makes a big difference. Say that you called a preflop raise with J♣ J♥ from a late position, and the flop comes A-J-6.

YOU

FLOP

Your opponent leads at the pot. You're pretty sure that he has a big ace or an overpair to your jacks such as kings or queens, so you don't try to shut him out. In this case, I would flat call his bet; I'm not going to move in on him at this point. Columbus took a chance, so I'm going to take one, too. If you're the first to act, you check to him. You see, in no-limit you're not trying to build a pot like you do in pot-limit, because the pot will take care of itself.

Say that the board pairs on fourth street, which strengthens your opponent's hand if it pairs one of the bottom cards on the board. If one of the top cards pairs, he's going to shut down anyway. If you had tried to shut him down on the flop, you would only have won what was already in the pot. But if any normal card comes off on the turn, he may bet again because you only flat called the flop. Then there are some chips in the pot and you have a chance to win some real money, so you can raise him to maximize what you can win on the hand.

The only thing that's going to beat you on this flop is a set of aces. If your opponent has flopped the aces, you're gone, of course—but you're going to play the hand anyway. In no-limit hold'em, it's very hard to get away from a set. But suppose your opponent bets, you raise, and he reraises you. You have to make a decision right there as to whether you have the best hand or only the second-best set. In a side game, it's hard to lay down your set, but in a tournament, it's easier to do. I've laid down sets, and I've seen other players do it too.

The Check-Call and the Flat Call

There is quite a difference between the check-call from a front position, and the flat call from a late position. When you're in a back position and just flat call a bet with a strong hand, it makes your hand appear to be weaker than when you check-call. This is true because a check-call will often ring a bell in your opponent's head and lead him to believe that you're slow playing, whereas a flat call from a late position is just everyday action and shouldn't set off any alarms in his mind.

The check-call is a little stronger than a flat call. So, in the situation discussed above, when you flop the set of jacks and are sitting in back of your opponent, you just flat call and hope that he bets again.

If he doesn't come again, you have two options: You can bet on fourth street, hoping that he will call; or you can wait until fifth street, which might weaken your hand in his eyes, and hope that your delayed bet will induce him to call. If he leads on fourth street, you might just call him again, unless he bets big, in which case you may want to shut him out right there. If he bets first on the river, then you come over the top of him. The whole idea is to extricate the most money out of his stack.

Now, let's look at a tournament hand in action that demonstrates some of the principles we've just discussed.

PLAYING A TROUBLE HAND IN TOURNAMENT ACTION

Ace-queen is a trouble hand that should be played with caution. During the first levels of play in a nine- or ten-handed game you don't want to put a lot of money in the pot with an A-Q (suited or unsuited) from an early position. Treat being suited as a bonus, something that should not change how you play the hand. Although I prefer suited cards when I play an A-Q, A-J or A-10, I value their ranks more than their suits.

Suppose you are in middle position during the second level of a $500 buy-in tournament. Nobody has entered the pot. You look down at the following:

YOU

You haven't caught a hand in quite a while, so you decide to raise to try to pick up the pot. An opponent reraises behind you. What do you do?

You fold. Why? Because you cannot stand a reraise before the flop with an A-Q in the opening rounds. Early in the tournament when I'm in middle to late position, if there are other limpers in the pot, I'll consider taking a cheap flop with the hand, but I won't raise with it. If there are no limpers, I like to bring it for a modest raise of about three times the size of the big blind. If anyone comes over the top of me, I fold.

If you catch either an ace or a queen on the flop, you will be in a bind as to what to do if someone bets at you. Why put yourself in that situation? You want to avoid having to make tricky decisions. For example, suppose the flop comes:

FLOP

You have flopped a queen and an early position raiser makes a big bet at the pot. Ask yourself what he could have, particularly if he's willing to jeopardize a lot of chips. People usually are not willing to risk getting broke early in a tournament unless they have a big pocket pair.

If I flop top pair and am the first to act, I usually will make a pot-sized bet on the flop, but if I get played with, I usually will shut down. In fact, it's easier to play *any* pair from up front than A-Q because a small to medium pair plays so easily after the flop—no set, no bet—whereas an A-Q or A-J require a lot of judgment if you get any action on the flop.

Later in the tournament, particularly when you're playing at a short-handed table, A-Q goes up in value. When you're either short-stacked or are up against a short stack, you might have to take a stand with the hand.

Another Trouble Hand, Another Tournament Problem

Now let's take a look at K-Q, a trouble hand that is weaker than A-Q. In no-limit hold'em, K-Q is a trap hand. Unless you flop J-10-9, A-J-10, two kings and a queen, or even two pair, you're in dire straits with this hand. The K-Q is a hand that you never want to play in a full ring game, in particular. The Q-J is the same type of hand. In fact, I give a little more value to the J-10 because you can make more straights with the hand than you can make with the K-Q or Q-J. I wouldn't stand a raise with J-10, but I might play it in late position.

Suppose you are playing in a $2,000 tournament and are dealt:

YOU

Situation 1

The action is passed to you on the button. What do you do? I treat K-Q like 2-3, like it's the plague in no-limit hold'em, unless everybody passes to me on the button. Then, I might raise the blinds with the hand, but that is the only place that I would raise with it.

Although K-Q suited is better than K-Q offsuit, being suited still doesn't change the fact that it can be a dangerous hand to play.

Situation 2

You are on the button with K-Q before the flop. A player raises in front of you. What do you do? I surely would not stand a raise with this hand or raise with it myself. Here is the trap that you get into.

Suppose you raise with the hand preflop and someone calls you. The flop comes:

YOU

FLOP

Now what are you going to do? You have top pair with second kicker. You don't have anything! There is a good chance that, since you were called before the flop, you are beaten already by someone who has an A-Q.

Situation 3

You are in the little blind with the K-Q. Everybody else has passed. What do you do? In this case, you can raise the big blind, even though you are out of position and will have to act first after the flop. Some players will call a small raise from the big blind with hands that aren't very good because they already have money in the pot, but the chances are good that you'll win the pot right there with your preflop raise.

OTHER TYPES OF HANDS AFTER THE FLOP

The next three chapters are devoted to playing special types of hands from preflop to finish in no-limit hold'em. In Chapter 6, "How to Win with Big Slick," we talk at length about playing A-K before and after the flop. We examine how to play small pairs and connectors in Chapter 7, before moving to Chapter 8 where we give you an in-depth analysis of playing dangerous draws.

6 HOW TO WIN WITH BIG SLICK

To win a no-limit tournament, you have to win with A-K and you have to beat A-K. You may not win or lose with it on the final hand, but it usually will be the deciding hand, the one that wins or loses the most chips for you. It's the biggest decision-hand in tournament poker.

More tournaments are won or lost with A-K against a big pair than any other hand. You might be up against two queens, flop an ace or a king, and win the pot, although the queens are an 11 to 10 favorite if you play 10,000 hands. But when you are running unlucky, it seems like somebody always catches up on the last two cards.

Early in the tournament, I treat A-K very softly. I might make a raise with it, but I'm not going to lose any more money if I don't flop pretty good to it. If someone raises from the front when I'm holding A-K in the back, the way I handle it largely depends on the player who makes the raise. There are times when I will just flat call the raise. There are times when I will try to win the money right then by reraising. And there are times when I will simply throw the hand away. It all depends on what I know about my opponent, and how he's playing that day.

RAISING AND RERAISING WITH A-K

Time and time again, I see players raise the pot with A-K in a full ring. Then somebody moves in on them and beats them for the pot. This is why I so often remind my seminar students that A-K is the most misplayed hand in no-limit poker.

The purpose of moving all-in before the flop is to see all five cards. I'm not a move-in player, but in certain situations (especially short-handed and late in the tournament) you may have to do it. Suppose a player raises, you call with A-K, and the flop comes 7-4-2.

YOU   **OPPONENT**

FLOP

Your opponent makes a bet—now you have to give up the hand. If you make a decision to play A-K short-handed, you move in with it because you want to see all the board cards. (Of course, you might be up against someone who is holding aces, and then you know you're in bad shape!)

I sometimes see a player with A-K call a reraise and get away with it, but I think that's a horrible play, because most of the time, the A-K is taking much the worst of it. With a decent amount of chips, this is an especially bad move. Why? Because when someone moves in on you after you have raised with A-K, you are *calling* all of your money with A-K. There is quite a difference in raising and calling with this hand.

On the button, you sometimes can reraise with A-K suited or even offsuit, but this type of raise is just a power play. In a power play, you raise enough money so that, hopefully, you can win the pot *before* the flop. You don't want to see the flop, but if you have to, you have to. And if you are forced to see it, chances are that you will have at least one or maybe two overcards on your opponents, so you're not dead. When you make this play, you're only hoping to win what is already in the pot.

The situation is different when you're playing short-handed. Then, A-K becomes a very powerful hand; A-Q becomes a powerful hand. The fewer the players, the less strength you usually will need to play. You also have other things working for you in short-handed play: Your chip position versus their chip position, and what money position both your opponents and you are in.

The second year that Johnny Chan won the World Series, when it was down to two tables, he played twelve times in 11 to 10 situations, either a big pair against two overcards or vice-versa—and he won all twelve times, which gave him chips for the final table. In his last hand against Frank Henderson, a similar situation came up. Johnny made a raise before the flop with A-9 and Henderson moved all-in. On the river came a 9 to beat Henderson's pocket fours.

PLAYING A-K AFTER THE FLOP

When the Flop Comes with Rags

Say that you have raised with A-K from a front spot and one or two people have called. The board comes 9-7-3, three suits. You are the first to act. What do you do with your A-K?

YOU

FLOP

I don't care whether or not I've raised before the flop, I never bet A-K when the flop comes with three rags. If you've raised the pot going in, your opponent(s) has some kind of hand or he wouldn't have called you. He didn't have a raising hand or he would have reraised before the flop, so you can put him on anything from queens on down in the pairs. He may even have an A-Q or A-J, but it is more likely that he holds a pair. Now, if you fire at this hand, he's liable to raise you or call you—and you don't have anything.

By betting, you have shut off your opportunity to get a free turn card and possibly make your hand. If you check-check, you have found out information without it costing you anything. An aggressive player like Phil Hellmuth may have a tendency to fire on the flop heads-up; that's his style of play. But you can burn up a lot of chips that way. I don't continue with A-K unless I flop a hand that relates to it in some way, a hand with some strength to it.

Same Situation, Different Position

Now, let's change the situation. The action is two-handed, but you're sitting *behind* the other player. The flop comes three rags. Your opponent checks to you. You are in the position of power. What's your best play?

YOU

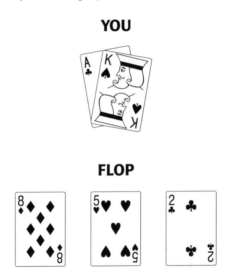

FLOP

You check right back at him. That way, you're not shutting yourself out. What will you do if he checks, you bet, and then he raises you? What are you going to do with your hand *then*? So, you may as well take the opportunity that his check has given you and get a free card by checking along.

On fourth street, you might hit an ace or king. If he checks again, you can fire at him. But once you don't hit your hand, put on the brakes and try to play a small pot. Hopefully, the other guy has an ace and you can play a showdown. If he bets, the most you can lose is your original raise. Or when he bets, you might decide that you have the best hand and call him. It all depends on the circumstances. But at least you have left all of your options open by checking along on the flop.

Someone suggested that this is an example of playing the waiting game. No, that's not it. This is an example of playing the hand the way that it *should* be played. Why take a chance and put all of your chips in jeopardy, especially in a tournament, when you don't have anything?

A lot of players will fire at the pot one time in these types of situations. When they see a baby flop, here they come! But I think they're making a mistake when they do that: You have to give an opponent credit for having something to have been able to call your raise to start with. If the board comes 9 high, he might have that board beaten; he might be in there with tens or jacks or queens, which aren't reraising hands anyway. You could be setting yourself up to lose a lot of money on the hand.

If a guy bets in front of me against that 9-high flop when I'm holding the A-K, he wins the pot. It's that simple. I don't *care* what he has—he wins it right there. As far as I'm concerned, A-K is A-K and two deuces beat A-K. It's a powerful hand if you can flop to it, but it isn't much of a hand when you don't.

Against an Ace-Rag-Rag Flop

Now suppose the flop comes A-6-3.

YOU

FLOP

Perfect! The only hands that you are afraid of on this flop are two aces in the hole, or two treys or two sixes in the hole, so you are definitely going to bet the hand. It is more likely that you'll run into exactly the type of hand that you want to go up against, an A-Q or A-J. You are not trying to shut your opponents out of the pot.

You don't mind if you opponent calls. You *want* a call. So, you want to bet enough to either win the pot right there or induce a call because, obviously, you are trying to maximize the amount that you can win on the hand.

If the board pairs the treys on the turn, that would be perfect. If he has A-Q or A-J, he probably will think, "I have a big kicker, so I'll call." And that's exactly what you want to happen. If your opponent has a trey or a set, you're already beaten anyway, and there's nothing that you can do about that.

When a Paint Comes on the Turn

As long as a picture card doesn't come on the board, you're in good shape. But if a picture card (a jack or a queen, for example) does come out after your opponent has called you on the flop, you had better shut down, because then you have a decision to make about the other player.

YOU

TURN

If he bets, the best hand you usually can have is a tie, with both of you holding an A-K. But there are a lot of other hands that he might have. You may be surprised at how many players will call you before the flop, and then not believe that you have an ace when an ace comes on the flop. An opponent may think that you're betting an underpair on the flop, and will call you with two queens or jacks in the hole. Then a queen comes off on the turn and, boy o' boy, you're in trouble. So, you must be very careful if a paint comes on fourth street.

When a paint doesn't come off, you want to make a fourth-street bet that is big enough to lose your opponent because you don't mind losing him at this point. You've already made money on the hand, and you don't want to give him a shot at making a double pair. So, you make a pretty good-sized bet on fourth street—if he calls, make him pay to do it.

A major axiom in no-limit hold'em is "Always make them pay to chase you." Bobby Hoff once said about me, "T. J. *will* make them look at their hole cards."

I suggest that you do the same thing.

Against a Drawing Hand

Even if an opponent has a drawing hand, you have distorted the pot so much that no drawing hand could be profitable. About the only type of drawing hand that could be out there on the A-6-3 flop is a 4-5. It is very unlikely that someone would be playing in a raised pot with a 4-5, but it does happen. You also come across certain players who will play any ace— A-6, A-4, A-8, and so on. But you *know* that about them, and take it into consideration.

In this example, if the river card is anything below a 10 without pairing the board again, you come at it with another bet. But once again, you should be very fearful if it comes with a queen or jack, or even a 10 in some situations. Of course, you should know which players will play 10-10 or A-10.

BIG SLICK IN ACTION

After studying each of the following hands, think about how you would play it. Then read the analysis that we give for the play of the hand and compare it with your ideas. In each example, Player A is the first to act; Player B is the next to act; and Player C is last to act.

Tournament Action Hand 1

At a no-limit tournament table, Player A raised $1,200 before the flop. You reraised $1,200. Player C cold called the reraise, and Player A called.

YOU

FLOP

Situation 1

Player A bets $8,000 on the flop. What is your best move?

I would have folded this hand before the flop if I had been you. But if you decide to play the hand, you should either flat call the $1,200 to see what comes on the flop, or raise about four times that amount (if you have enough chips). You want to put in a big enough raise to shut out the rest of the field so that you can play heads-up against one opponent.

If you make a large raise, the original raiser may:

> **(a)** throw his hand away and you will win the pot right there, or
>
> **(b)** call

In either case, your raise probably will freeze out the rest of the field.

But you didn't do that. You let Player C into the pot (who even cold called your raise), so you have to give both Player C and Player A credit for having good hands.

Why would I throw the hand away when Player A bets $8,000 on the flop? For two reasons: First of all, Player A has A-A, A-K, Q-Q, or A-Q. Or if he's a loose player, he could have two sevens in his hand. Since I have the K♠ in my hand, I don't put him on a spade draw. Secondly, since Player C cold called behind me, he also could have flopped a set. Therefore, I would fold the A-K.

Situation 2

Player A checks on the flop. What do you do?

You also check.

Situation 3

Player A moves all-in on the flop. What is your best move?

Pass.

Analysis

Some of the key elements for analysis that are missing from this scenario are the number of players who are at the table; whether this hand comes up in the early, middle, or late stage of the tournament; and how much you know about your opponents.

Because you have been studying the game while you were playing, you should know which players will raise or reraise with A-J or A-Q, and which players will not raise unless they have aces or kings. If your opponent is the type of player who won't raise with a weak hand, you don't have anything with the A-K, so why not get rid of it?

Now, suppose you have $2,500 in front of you, and you bring it in for $1,500. Then somebody reraises behind you. You are pot-committed and you go on with the play because you have more than one-half of your chips already in the pot. An experienced player often will pot-commit himself by putting in most of his chips when he raises because he knows that if he gets reraised, he will automatically go for the rest of it. A less experienced player might think that he can blow the raiser off the hand by reraising. He mistakenly believes that the raiser will save that extra $500 or $1,000 that he has left.

What the inexperienced reraiser doesn't realize is that the only reason that the raiser has pot-committed himself is so that he cannot get away from the hand.

Tournament Action Hand 2

This time, let's fill in some of the missing elements from Action Hand One. You are playing in a $1,000 buy-in tournament. It is in the middle stage of the tournament and you are playing at a full table.

Player A raises $1,200 before the flop. You are Player B sitting in fifth position with four players behind you. You reraise $4,800. Player C cold calls the reraise for $6,000. Player A also calls. You hold the same hand as before.

YOU

FLOP

Situation 1

Player A checks on the flop. What's your best move?

You are in a quandary. You have top pair and the nut flush draw, and there is $18,000 in the pot. This could be the perfect trap hand, but you have to play it, so you move in with all of your chips. If you're up against a set, of course, you can't beat it, but still, you're drawing to the nut flush. It doesn't matter what Player C does—you are playing the hand.

Situation 2

Player A bets. What do you do?

Again, you move all in. You can't hope for a better flop, unless it had come A-A-K. This is a flop that you have to play.

Tournament Action Hand 3

Once again, you have been dealt Big Slick. The tournament conditions and preflop action are the same as in Action Hand Two. Player A raises $1,200 before the flop. You are sitting in fifth position with four players behind you. You reraise $4,800. Player C cold calls the reraise for $6,000. Player A also calls.

YOU

FLOP

Situation 1

Player A bets. Your observation has told you that Player A is a pretty good player. What do you do with your A-K?

Pass. A lot of times, good players will move with a big hand in the hope that you will play back at them. Since you know that Player A is a strong player, throw the hand away.

Situation 2

Player A checks. Now what do you do?

You also check. Then, if Player C bets, you throw the hand away.

Analysis

Tossing your hand is tough to do because you have a lot of money in the pot. But why give up the tournament for this one hand? The A-K is a perfect trap hand, unless you're playing at a short-handed table. Short-handed, it becomes a powerful hand. If you're playing against five or fewer players, A-K is a strong hand, but when you're playing in a full ring, there are a lot of situations when Big Slick amounts to nothing. You want to avoid any traps that you might get into with it.

Two queens is a decent raising hand, one that a lot of players will stand a reraise with. Therefore, given this flop, there is a good chance that either Player A or Player C has flopped quad queens—or a full house if either one is holding A-Q.

People think that Big Slick is such a big-big hand, but it isn't. Two deuces is a better hand than A-K. In a computer run of 100,000 hands, two deuces will win more often than A-K in heads-up situations played to a showdown.

Tournament Action Hand 4

You have Big Slick, the same hand that you held in the last three Action Hands. But this time, the flop comes with three baby cards.

YOU

FLOP

Situation 1

Player A bets. What do you do?

You throw your hand away. Why? Because you have nothing. In no-limit hold'em, you never chase.

Situation 2

Player A checks. What's your move?

You also check.

Situation 3

Player A checks. You check. Player C bets. What's your best move?

You fold, no matter what Player A does after Player C bets. Again, you never chase with A-K in no-limit hold'em.

Analysis

Remember that Player C cold called a reraise before the flop and has position on you. It's fairly certain that he can beat a pair of deuces, fours, or sevens—and your A-K can't beat any of those pairs—one more reason to dump your A-K if he bets.

HOW TO WIN WITH SMALL PAIRS AND CONNECTORS

In Dallas, when a player used to show down his hand and say, "I've got one small pair," it usually was two queens! Of course, that is no longer true. When we say "small pair" these days, we usually mean any pair lower than 8-8. Middle pairs are 10-10, 9-9, and 8-8. Small pairs are 7-7, 6-6, 5-5 and lower. I even call 4-4, 3-3 and 2-2 baby pairs. But really, that much differentiation isn't necessary.

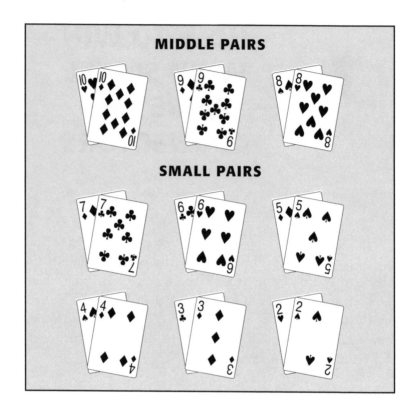

SMALL PAIRS BEFORE THE FLOP

Tom and I have different opinions on how to play the small pairs. We're going to discuss both of our points of view in this section to give you a broader spectrum of choices for your own playing style.

McEvoy's Pov

Tom likes to limp in with the small pairs, tens on down to deuces, even from a front position. He sees them as strictly limping hands, unless he decides to take a shot at the blinds with them from a middle position on back, in which case he might bring them in for a small raise. He likes to mix up his play with them like this in a full ring.

Occasionally, he also will bring in the pot for a small raise with a pair such as sixes from a front position if he is the first one in the pot. If someone pops him with a modest raise and it looks like he'll be playing head-up, he mucks them. But if the reraiser makes a small raise with a lot of chips in front of him, Tom will call with a small pair in hope of flopping a set, knowing that most of the time, he will have to give them up.

If one or two players in the ring have been doing a lot of preflop raising, Tom will just pass with the small pairs.

Usually, it is in the early stages of the tournament when there is still a lot of limping going on that he will slip in with them because he thinks that small pairs play the easiest of any other starting hand. If he doesn't flop a set, he can easily get away from them, although he may give some action if he flops an open-ended straight draw. In no-limit, there are huge implied odds, especially in the early rounds when everybody has a lot of chips in relation to the size of the blinds. Tom isn't looking for a big pot in the first round of the tournament unless he has the nuts or close to it and he is looking to trap somebody who is holding a big hand such as aces or another big pair or a set.

Cloutier's Pov

In contrast, I am not going to play little pairs, eights and below, in the first three or four seats in a full ring. If I play them at all, I will only play them from the next five seats, and I am not going to raise with them in a full ring. First of all, I don't want to give away any information about my hand. When you're playing a small pair and there are two callers behind you, there is the chance that they might each have a pair or two big connectors, normal playing hands.

The reason for not raising with your small pair is that you hope to flop a set. You're not risking much money by just calling; and if you get raised, you can get rid of your hand. The perfect situation is when you hold a pair of eights and the flop comes K-8-2. If your opponents are playing their hands strong, you can set them up pretty well against this type of flop.

I don't play small pairs in early position because I think that I will just be giving away my money. A lot of pots are raised in no-limit hold'em; very few are limp-limp-limp. You cannot stand a raise with the small pairs, especially early in the tournament. In the first part of the tournament, you have x-amount of dollars, and every dollar that you lose in a pot is a drain on chips that you could have used later to double or triple up when you have a big hand. I think along these lines all of the time. If anything, I might play the small pairs later in the tournament rather than early.

Suppose the blinds are $50 and I bring it in for $50. Then somebody raises me $150 and I decide to take a shot at it. On the flop, I don't like my hand and have to give it up. Now I've wasted $200. Later on when I have a big hand with, maybe, two-way action, I could have turned that $200 into $600. That's how you accumulate chips in a tournament.

I do not play baby pairs, but I might just flat call with a pair of eights or better from early position, hoping that I don't get raised. If I get raised, I just throw them away, since I only have a minimum amount in the pot. One big tournament winner that I know likes to come in with a raise before the flop with little pairs, hoping that he will flop a set that nobody will put him on, and hoping that he won't get blown off the hand by a big raise behind him. It's a risk that he's willing to take.

Just remember that you cannot handle any heat with the small pairs before the flop.

Some top players don't mind limping in with the small pairs or bringing them in for a small raise. They will stand a small raise and try to catch a set on the flop. Say that Player A brings it in for $50 and someone makes it $150 or $200. If Player A has $5,000 or more chips in front of him, he might call the raise, but will give no further action on the flop unless he flops the set. I very seldom do that.

I want to take out a player, just like everyone else does, but if I'm going to play a small pair, I don't want to play it against only one opponent; I want to play it in a multiway pot. Then if I make a set, I might really make some money on the hand. I don't understand why a person would play small pairs head-up, when they know that they are a dog to start with. The time to play the small pairs is when you are in late position or when you are in a short-handed game.

Neither Tom's method nor mine is the gospel truth on playing small pairs. I am simply thinking along different lines when I play them. Tom is willing to take a risk with small pairs and even call a small raise with them. In situations where I am looking to save some bets, Tom is more willing to gamble a little bit. There certainly are more than two ways to play in almost every situation.

SMALL PAIRS AFTER THE FLOP

How you play small pairs after the flop depends upon the texture of the flop. Say that you took the flop with 4-4. You called a small raise or maybe two or three players limped in, probably with face cards. The flop comes 9-7-4.

YOU

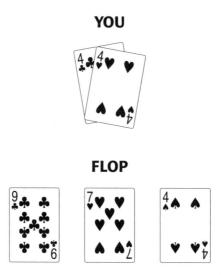

FLOP

What's your best play?

This is not a pot that you want to lead at because you want your opponents to catch up with you somewhat. If they all check, that's fine. You're hoping that a face card will hit on the turn so that you can get some action.

Now, suppose the flop comes K-Q-4.

YOU

FLOP

What's your best play on this flop?

In this case, you have to play completely differently. This is a dangerous flop for you with your bottom set. If somebody with pocket kings or queens raised the pot before the flop, you have to be very careful with the hand. You may think that you have the best hand, but that isn't necessarily true. You have to let your opponents' betting patterns and how they play the hand dictate the way that you play the hand.

In an unraised pot, you can be less fearful that someone has limped in with pocket kings or queens, but in a raised pot there is always the danger that your opponent has raised with the big pocket pairs. In an unraised pot, you can be 99 percent sure that you have the best hand, although someone occasionally will limp with kings or queens in the hole. This type of trap flop is just one more reason why I don't like to play baby pairs in early position. I realize that set over set doesn't come up very often, but it does happen. And when it happens, it will destroy you if you hold the low set.

I remember a hand that I played three-handed in a side game in Dallas against Bobby Hoff and Herschel from Houston. Herschel had raised ten pots in a row with anything from pocket deuces on up, but he limped into this pot. Bobby was on the button and he made a little raise (any time he's on the button, he makes a little courtesy raise). I was in the blind with two fours in the hole and decided to call. Herschel also called. The flop came 10-6-4. I checked, Herschel checked, and Bobby bet on the button. I knew that he had an overpair, because he would have checked if he hadn't hit it. Then I raised. Herschel reraised.

When Herschel reraised, he could have had anything, an overpair or something like that. Bobby studied for a long time, and then he folded his two queens. I was completely pot committed. Out of $5,000, I had $1,000 left in front of me. I called Herschel's reraise. He had limped in with 10-10. This is the perfect example of a situation in which you can get trapped. My play was fine, but I was a gone goose.

In Jeopardy with a Small Pair

You're always taking a chance of getting into jeopardy with the small pairs. Say that you are in the pot with pocket fours. The flop comes 2-3-5.

YOU

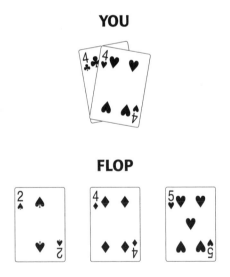

FLOP

Now how are you going to play the hand?

You have second pair and an open-ended straight draw. Someone might play this hand, and sometimes play it very strongly, and never get there. Tom says that in this situation, he will check so that no on can raise him off the hand. Then if somebody bets at it, he might come back with a raise.

But say that you lead with a pot-sized bet and somebody moves in on you. In a tournament, you cannot call, whereas in a side game, you might make the call or even lead at the pot. That's the difference between the two.

In my opinion, there are so many traps that you can fall into with small pairs that I play them very carefully. There may be even more traps when you play the suited connectors than there are with small pairs, but of course, there are a lot of connectors that you never play.

PLAYING SUITED CARDS

Suited cards are what I refer to as "A Broke's Lament." As he leaves the table, a guy tells his buddy, "I got busted in this pot, but I was suited."

Players like that put tremendous value in holding two suited cards, the K♣ 5♣ or the A♥ 6♥. Believe me, the value in these hands is very slim unless you flop a flush to them, but some players will even call raises with them! With these types of hands, what do you want to hit except for a flush?

As far as I'm concerned, the only value in suited cards occurs when you are holding A-K, A-Q, or A-J. Being suited gives them a little extra added value. Their real value is in their ranks. Actually I am just as happy with unsuited A-K or A-Q or A-J as I am when they are suited. If you would not play any two cards unsuited, you have no reason to play them suited.

Suppose you're holding the K-Q suited and make a flush on the flop. Since your opponents probably have no redraws on an unpaired board, you win only what is in the pot if you bet it from up front. In actual play, the hand is over at that point. Therefore, you have to check your flush from a front spot to slow down the action a little bit. Certainly, if your opponent makes a bet, you might raise him, although I may be more inclined to just flat call him, because I don't want to have to decide whether or not to play the hand for all my money. Also, you might be up against a bigger flush if your opponent has the ace-suited in his hand.

So, you always want to try to play these types of hands from a back position so that you will have more betting options. Personally, the big suited cards, A-K through A-J, are the only types of suited hands that I want to play. With the lower suited cards, you might make a flush, but your opponent may make a bigger flush. Certainly, you wouldn't play A-little suited; I don't even play it in limit hold'em.

A Rule for Suited Cards

The general rule is: If you wouldn't play any two cards unsuited, you should not play them suited. Of course, there are a few exceptions. For example, if several players have trailed into an unraised pot and you are on the button with king-small suited, you might call the pot in the hope of flopping the big flush. You never would call a raise, however.

The danger with playing this type of hand is that you might flop top pair, have the action checked to you, and then feel "forced" to make a little bet at the pot. You're leaving yourself wide open to a check-raise and may wind up losing money with a hand that you shouldn't have played in the first place. Because of the likelihood of this happening, I don't want to play hands like that; I don't want to put myself in that spot.

PLAYING THE SMALL CONNECTORS

When is it correct to call a raise with small connectors? Answer: When you are on the button or in the spot right in front of the button, with a lot of chips against a lot of chips. In this situation, there is nothing wrong with calling a small raise with 4-5 suited, 6-7 suited, or 7-8 suited. Your opponents will never put you on this type of hand to start with, and if you don't flop to it, you can get rid of it right away. You're simply taking a shot at busting somebody with your small suited connectors.

You can call a raise in multiway pots in this type of scenario, and you sometimes can do it heads-up in a big-stack against big-stack situation. But those are the only times that I am going to play small connectors; I am never going to open a pot with them.

What if you flop a draw to this type of hand? To repeat, I try to stay away from as many draws in no-limit hold'em as I possibly can, especially in tournaments. In tournaments, *draws are death*. You're always taking the worst of it when you're taking a draw; you know that you're always the underdog when you call a bet to draw to your hand.

For example, say that the board comes 2-3-10 and you have stood a little raise before the flop with 4-5 in a late position.

YOU

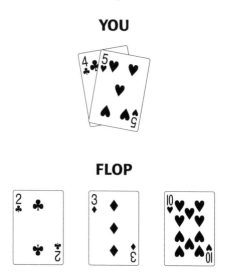

FLOP

Somebody makes a bet at you. I would never flat call with this drawing hand against a bet. I would either raise him right on the flop to try to blow him out of the pot, or fold. Why? Because if you don't make the draw on the first card off, he's going to come after you again and then you will have to dump your hand. With these types of connectors, your decision *always comes on the flop.*

Now suppose you hold this same 4-5 and several people are in the pot. The original bettor bets at the pot, someone calls, and then it's up to you. What do you do? Nothing has changed. If you make a play at the pot (raise) and blow both of them off, you will simply win double money. But you're taking the chance of getting called, and then you will have nothing. That is why I either fold the hand, or make the raise.

If Player A bets and Player B calls, what do I have with the 4-5 on the 2-3-10 flop? I have eight outs twice if my cards are still in the deck—if neither of them is holding two aces or two sixes. But I am not looking to get pot odds in a no-limit tournament. Anytime you make a play in a tournament and get beaten for all of your chips, you're out of action. This thought always has to be in the back of your mind, though it shouldn't be a fear factor that keeps you from making correct plays. If you have fear in no-limit hold'em, you'd better not play the game.

Now suppose you have J-10 in your hand and the flop comes 8-9-2.

YOU

FLOP

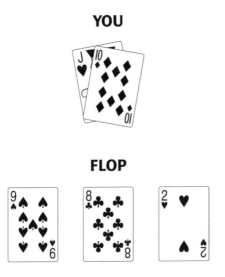

There is some strength in this hand: You have two overcards and the top straight draw. This is the type of overlay situation that you are looking for on your drawing hands. But the other question to consider if the board comes 9 high is, "Do I have two overcards and a straight draw?"

Here's another example of suited connectors. This time the blinds are $25/$50 and you're in the early stages of a tournament: You are in sixth position with the 6♦ 5♦, and two limpers are in the pot.

YOU

If you don't think that you will be raised, you can call with this hand. This example illustrates Tom's two-limper rule in limit hold'em, which also applies somewhat in no-limit play.

If you limp with this hand in limit hold'em, and the pot is raised only one unit, you can call the raise; but in no-limit, if someone puts in a pot-sized raise before the flop, you dump the hand when you are out of position. If you are only slightly out of position in no-limit, say the sixth spot, and no one raises the pot, you can limp with the hand. This is a situation where "feel" comes into the game.

Now let's analyze a few hands in tournament action to see how these principles apply at the table.

Tournament Action Hand 1

At last, you have made it to the final table in a no-limit hold'em tournament. The table is six-handed, and you look down at this hand on the button: 6♥ 6♠

YOU

The action is passed to you. What do you do?

A very famous tournament player that I know has a favorite move at the final table of a tournament—and there are a lot of players who use this same move. When they are around back and have a pair of fives or sixes, for example, they invariably move in their whole stacks when it is passed to them. I think that this is the most horrible play that I have ever seen in hold'em.

When you have worked that hard to get to the final table, why take the chance of losing your whole stack with a small pair? If the first four of five players in front of you don't have anything, there's a decent chance that one of the players behind you *will* have something. I have seen it happen time and time again: A player loses his entire stack because he moves in with all of his chips.

In this situation, it might be okay to make a baby raise, or even a decent-sized raise. For example, say that the antes are $200 and the blinds are $400/$800 at a six-handed table. There is $2,400 in the pot. You have $15,000 in front of you. If you want to raise, why not bring it in for $3,000? That's plenty—if you get reraised, you can get away from the hand; if you get outflopped, you can get away from it. But what are you going to do if you move in your whole stack and get called?

I often hear players talk about the A-K being only an 11 to 10 underdog to a pair. But what they don't realize is that if you have two sixes, for example, and your opponent has a 7-8, the 7-8 also is only an 11 to 10 dog to your pair of sixes. It isn't just the A-K that is the underdog: *Any* two overcards are only an 11 to 10 underdog to a pair. And if the overcards are suited, they are a slightly smaller dog to the pair. These numbers are what make moving in your whole stack with a small pair such a horrible play.

Sometimes, of course, those small pairs come through for you. Here's a famous example of 6-6 beating Big Slick.

Tournament Action at the 1993 World Series

At the final table of the 1993 World Series of Poker, John Bonetti, Jim Bechtel, and Glenn Cozen were playing three-handed at the final table. Bonetti raised before the flop with A-K and Cozen folded. Playing three-handed, Bechtel did what he was supposed to do: He called with pocket sixes. The flop came with a 6 and a king in it. Bonetti bet and Bechtel flat called him.

If you know your players, Bechtel's flat call in this situation is the single biggest tell in the world. Jim Bechtel is a great player, and I know that he plays all of his big hands from behind. He lets you get yourself involved before he does anything. His hands are weaker when he is leading than when he is check-calling. The worst hand that he could have had in this situation was an A-K to tie with Bonetti.

Phil Hellmuth and I were watching the action on the TV monitor when this hand came up. When Bonetti bet and Bechtel just called, I said to Phil, "Bonetti had better shut down right now." But he didn't. He moved in his whole stack on the turn. Bechtel won the hand, of course, and Bonetti came in third to Cozen.

Tournament Action Hand 2

YOU

If you're getting three or four callers in a raised pot and you're sitting around back with a lot of chips, obviously you like your pocket fours. But playing heads-up or even a three-way pot isn't a good idea with these little pairs. From a front position, I throw pocket fours away as though they were 7-2.

Can you ever stand a raise with baby pairs? Only if you're getting very good pot odds. Obviously you're hoping to flop a set and rake in a good pot. But if you don't flop a set to your little pair, there are very few scenarios where you can play them. In other words, you need to get very lucky to win with small pairs.

Small pairs are takeoff hands in no-limit when you have a lot of chips. Keep in mind that 4-4 is only an 11-10 favorite over a 6-5. When you take that into account, there are a lot of hands better than two fours. Pocket fives have a little more value because the 5 is a straight card.

Yet time and time again you see players who don't have very many chips play these hands, even though they're not out of contention yet. They have $3,000 in chips, look down at a baby pair, and move all in. An opponent calls and the flop comes with an A-K. At the most they are an 11 to 10 favorite or they're a 4.5 to 1 dog. Of course if you're anteing more than $200 or so, and you have $800 with the blinds coming up, that's a different situation. In that situation, you might play the hand. But with $3,000 or $4,000 in chips, you have time to wait for a better hand.

While there are certain situations when you can play small pocket pairs, I recommend that you usually avoid them. If you stand a little raise in no-limit with a baby pair, it's almost always because you have huge implied odds, lots of chips to play in comparison to your opponents, and you're getting multiway action. Playing hands like 4-4 heads-up for a raise, however, is almost always a mistake. And people who move in with these types of hands are just asking to get broke.

Tournament Action Hand 3

YOU

The 9-8 suited is an interesting hand in that it has a lot of potential to be a takeoff hand in the right situations, but it is a chip burner if it is not played properly.

Middle connectors are hands that you play in side games to try to take somebody off. In tournaments, one big drawback is always staring you in the face—you can't go back to your pocket when you lose all your chips.

MIDDLE CONNECTORS IN EARLY POSITION

Playing a 9-8 suited or offsuit is an absolute no-no in early position because the hand cannot stand any pressure. The chips you do not lose on bad hands will be available to you later to possibly double or triple up with on your good hands. It's hell to lose a lot of chips on lousy hands, finally wake up with a hand, double up with it, and then find yourself right back where you started, rather than being ahead. You have to think about all these things in tournament play—and especially when you're considering playing hands such as 9-8 or 8-7 or 7-6 suited from up front.

If you think of playing middle connectors in no-limit hold'em like you would play them in Omaha, you know that any time you only flop an open-ended straight draw, you don't bet it. If you had some other outs in addition to the straight, you might call a bet. Implant this same kind of thinking in your head when you decide to play middle connectors in no-limit hold'em and flop to them. You know that if you get played with, your opponent probably has a draw-out hand.

You want to play small pots with middle suited connectors, not big pots. Therefore, you don't lead with drawing hands unless you are prepared to stand a raise, as is the case when you have a straight draw, a flush draw, and two overcards to the board. Take a look:

YOU

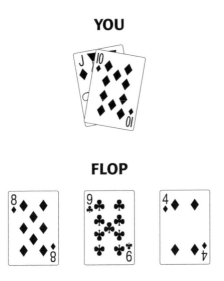

FLOP

You also can lead if you happen to flop a straight, two pair or a set. If a good card comes for you on fourth street, then play it strong, but don't get involved early. Give yourself a chance to get away from the hand.

Late Position

When two or more limpers have entered the pot, you might occasionally play middle connectors from the cutoff seat or the button.

Suppose everyone passes to you on the button and you have the 9♥ 8♥. What do you do? Fold. Remember that if nobody in front of you has a hand, somebody behind you might have one. McEvoy calls it the "bunching factor," meaning that if no one has big cards in front of you, it is somewhat more likely that big cards are "bunched" behind you.

Some people like to limp with middle connectors in this situation, but what are you trying to accomplish when you do that? If nobody has called before you and you limp from the cutoff seat or the button, where is the value in the hand? If either the button or the small blind call, you could be a big dog in the hand. And if only the big blind plays, even if he only holds a hand as weak as 10-2 offsuit, he's still a favorite over you.

Now suppose you have 9-8 in the small blind and everybody has passed. Naturally you call for one-half a bet. If you get raised, of course you throw the hand away.

The only time that I see value in middle-connector hands such as 9♣ 8♣ in no-limit hold'em is when you hold them in the big blind in an unraised pot, or when you call for one-half a bet from the small blind. If the flop comes 9 high, you're not going to play aggressively. Remember that there are a lot of people who play ace-anything—A-9, A-10, A-8—for the minimum bet. Sure, any two cards can win in poker, but that doesn't mean you should play them.

HOW TO DODGE DANGEROUS DRAWS IN TOURNAMENTS

Players make more mistakes with drawing hands than any other type of hand. At the World Poker Tour boot camps that I teach, we talk a lot about the odds, the outs, and other mathematics concepts. Most people accept 28 wins with two to go—that's 14 outs twice—as an even hand in no-limit hold'em. In other words, you can catch 14 cards on fourth street and 14 more on fifth street, 28 outs on the draw, to beat a hand that already has you beaten on the flop.

Say you have J-10 offsuit in your hand and the board comes 9-8-2.

YOU

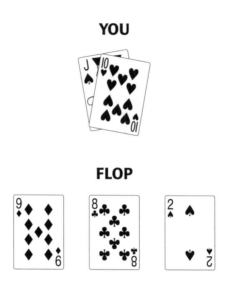

FLOP

You have two overs and a straight draw, so you have 8 straight cards you can win with (4 queens and 4 sevens), and you can catch a jack (3 outs) or a 10 (3 outs) to make top pair. Now you have 4 + 4 + 3 + 3 x 2, or 14 outs twice, once on the turn and once on the river. You have what's known as "an even hand with two to come." But that's an even hand, and you have to make your hand and they already have theirs. In a cash game, you have a good play. In a tournament when your life is on the line, you have a bad play that you simply cannot make.

With an open-end straight draw and a flush draw, you have what's known as 15 wins twice against any other hand. You have 8 straight cards to make your straight, plus 7 cards to make a flush. (You don't have 9 cards to make your flush, since 2 flush cards have already been counted as straight cards.)

Let's say that you have 15 wins twice against an overpair or two pair. You'll have a complete hand if you make it. So you have 30 outs, 15 outs twice, making you a 30 to 28 favorite. If you're playing in a cash game, you play this type of hand.

Why? Because you know that even if you miss your draw, you can put more money on the table and stay in action.

PLAYING A DRAWING HAND BEFORE THE FLOP

However, you do not get yourself into these situations in a tournament. When you are dealt this type of hand, you have to factor your chip standing at the time, your position—all those considerations—into your decision. If your stack is so short that you have to play something—in other words, you're forced to gamble—you might play your drawing hand.

Now, let's say that you have an average stack and it's late in the tournament. If you play this hand, you have to be willing to put all your money into the pot. Why? Because if you don't make it on fourth street, your opponent will more than likely bet so big that it's not poker to call. And then you've lost all that money. So, you must be careful in making decisions about drawing hands.

Sure, you're a favorite at 30 to 28, but those odds are calculated over a million hands. What happens if those odds and those outs don't kick in for the first 200,000 hands you're dealt—and then they play out in your favor five times in a row when you complete your draw? See what I'm saying here if the odds don't kick in early? The odds are the same every single time you make the draw, but that doesn't mean it's going to happen right then. It could happen at some other time, but not then.

So, if you know your tournament life is on the line if you draw, you don't draw when you have an average stack. Remember that no-limit hold'em is 99.9 percent pure discipline and common sense. Common sense is one of the most underrated things in poker. Try saying something like this to yourself: "If I make this draw, I'm going to win this pot. But if I lose this draw, I'm in deep trouble."

Sure, I play a drawing hand once in a while—in certain situations. If you get down to less than ten big blinds in your stack, you're looking for anything to get your money in with. But why take a chance otherwise? When you're right on the curve for that stage of the tournament, why would you want to blow a lot of your money on the draw?

Your chip stack really has a bearing on what your can do in a tournament. If you're in late position and you have plenty of chips, you can play the drawing hands in a multiway pot where you'll have a good chance of getting paid off if you make it. There's a whole lot of money in multiway pots to start with, more than just what you could make by doubling up against a single opponent. You want to get money from as many opponents as you can. This is where position comes into the spotlight in hold'em. You have to be smart about it.

Playing "If-Come" on the Flop

The most outs you can have on a draw is 42 (21 twice). That happens when you have two overcards (6 outs), a straight draw (8 outs) and a flush draw (7 outs) on the flop against top pair. It's a freakish hand when it comes up. It might look something like this:

YOU

FLOP

At 42 to 28, you're a 3 to 2 favorite. If it's passed to you on the flop, you might as well lead with the hand because you're not going to fold even if you get raised.

You have a powerhouse draw. But wait—it's got to hit! And your opponent already has a hand. How many times have you had the odds in your favor, and the board pairs or it comes deuce-trey? Even with all these outs, you're still on what we call the "if-come." And that can be very dangerous, especially since you almost always have considerably fewer outs.

Another element has to be added to this mix. Let's say that you have 15 outs twice (a straight draw and a flush draw). If you make your hand on the first card, and you're not already all-in, is your opponent going to pay you off? You're taking a calculated chance to make it on the if-come, but will you get paid off if you're successful? He can see the possibilities on the board just as well as you can. This is a big factor.

Your opponents are plenty good enough these days to know that when a certain card comes, it can really hurt them. They can figure out the possibilities of your hand when you play it. So now you make the damn thing, and you don't get paid off. You've taken a big chance and you haven't made any more money than what was already in the pot. Doesn't make much sense to try it, does it?

Now let's say that you have an open-end straight draw and a flush draw and your opponent has the nut flush draw. He doesn't have a pair or an overpair or two pair, he has the nut flush draw. So now, even if you make the flush draw, you lose. In that case, you're dead to the straight, so you have half the outs you thought you had. When you have only a flush draw, be sure you have the nut flush draw. Otherwise you're drawing dead if you and your opponent both hit the flush.

Suppose the pot is multiway, you're in late position where you can't get rehashed, and you can make the draw on the cheap. In this case, you can play it. But if you're in early position and you lead at the pot with your flush draw, somebody's probably going to raise you, and then you're right back in the black pit I just described.

PLAYING A DRAW ON FOURTH STREET

Suppose you're in a multiway pot and everybody checks around to you on fourth street. You've picked up a draw with one card to come, and you're the last to act. You can get a free card since everybody has checked to you. Even if you have a straight draw and a flush draw, you cannot bet this hand! If you bet on the come, somebody can raise and knock you off the hand. You've just wasted money by betting. For example, say that you have the J♣ 10♣.

On fourth street the board is showing 9-8-2-4 with two clubs.

YOU

BOARD

It looks like you have the Holy City, but all you really have is a draw and a jack high. If you bet on the if-come, you will be giving your opponents a chance to blow you out of the pot. What happens if you bet and somebody check-raises? It will cost you a lot of money to call with one card to come. You might even have to dump the hand! You've committed the cardinal sin of no-limit hold'em with drawing hands. You've put a double-barreled whammy on yourself. You've wasted all that money and wasted the chance to catch your card.

Now let's say that you throw caution to the wind and bet the hand. Nobody raises, but one player calls. You make your hand on fifth street. Your bet on the turn told your opponent that you have a pretty decent hand.

The result?

Even when you're successful, you might not make anything on the end. See what I mean? There's a big difference between checking and betting on the turn. When you check along on the turn, you don't put yourself in any jeopardy, and you don't give anybody any clues about the strength of your hand. Then when you catch your card on fifth street, your opponents don't know where you are in the hand because you haven't given them any information.

HOW TO MASTER EACH STAGE OF TOURNAMENTS

In tournament play, you have to survive long enough to have a chance to win. Survive early, win at the end. Even though some people may be playing crazy and a few players are winning a lot of chips that way, keep only one goal in your mind at all times—winning the tournament.

THE EARLY STAGE

You can't win it in the first hour, or in the first two or three hours. First you have to outlast the other players. That is why you don't want to open up too much during the first three, four or five hours of the tournament. You want to play solid and let your opponents make the mistakes. You will be playing your perfect ring-game strategy.

During the early rounds in particular, good tournament players stay away from the types of drawing hands we discussed in Chapter 8. However, situations do come up in which you must play a draw. Suppose you have raised the pot with Big Slick and the board comes with rags, two of which are in your suit.

YOU

FLOP

Follow the classic seven-card stud strategy: Don't draw at a flush unless you have two overcards to the board and are drawing to the nut flush. When you have two overcards and the nut-flush draw, you have a huge hand. In fact, it is the only type of flush draw that I want to play because the hand has so many outs. In the situation pictured above, you can hit either an ace or a king, either one of which will give you top pair/top kicker, and any heart to make the nut flush and win the hand.

Playing a common flush draw in the early stages of the tournament is foolish. Some weaker players will get involved with a flush draw and put one-half of their chips in the pot with their chances of making the flush only 1 in 3. Sometimes, they will make the flush and still lose to the nut flush. A lot of players make this error, but the top players *never* make this mistake.

It is almost always the weak players who put the beats on you, not the strong ones who are playing sensibly. Of course, if it weren't for weak players, we wouldn't have such huge overlays in the World Series of Poker. But it's very frustrating to see a bad player make a bad play such as putting all of his money in with the 9♣ 8♣, get there, and knock you off on the river with a drawing hand he shouldn't have been playing in the first place. You know that this type of player has zero chance of winning the tournament, but he can totally eliminate *your* chances.

The Maze

I think that you should treat tournament poker like you would a maze that has nothing but trap doors at every turn. You always have to be careful to stay out of those traps, dodging the land mines. You want to be an offensive poker player who plays defense naturally. Thinking along these lines should be second nature to you.

If you don't have anything at all on the flop, somebody can pick up on that and be sharp enough to shut you out on the turn. But if you use your common sense and don't take that first card off with a mediocre hand, you won't waste a lot of precious chips. Once again, play *survival*. In the flush-draw discussed above, you don't let anybody shut you out because you're the one who's putting the money in the pot. You fully commit yourself to the hand.

In the early stages, you don't want to make a lot of sudden moves; you just have to play a patient, controlled game while looking for a few openings to put up some chips. While you should play more conservatively in the opening rounds, you don't need to play so tight that you don't take enough risks

MIDDLE STAGE

There is no cut and dried formula as to when you start opening up your play in a tournament. You have to size up the table that you're on, assess how your opponents are playing in different situations. By the time you get to the middle stage, you should know which players are moving in which situations, which players are likely to call you and which ones are not.

You also know that the worst play you can make is to bluff at a bad player. Bad players will not lay down a hand, even in a tournament. If you're going to run a bluff, run it at a good player because he's not afraid to lay down a hand.

In the first round when the blinds are relatively small, there may be some occasions when you can bluff, but mostly, you're just waiting for a good hand and the right opening to try to trap your opponents. Usually, you're waiting to trap the weak players, not the strong ones—the strong ones are waiting to do exactly the same thing to you!

Opening Up Your Play

In the middle rounds, you can start to play semi-aggressively, opening up your play and stepping up your action a notch or two. In this middle stage, around the fourth or fifth level, the big blinds are about $200 in the big events. At this point, about one-half of the field has been eliminated, and the remaining players are beginning to accumulate chips. Say that you have inched up the size of your stack from your original $2,000 in chips to $2,500. Unfortunately, with only a 25 percent increase in your stack size, you have a sub-standard stack. You can't just sit there and play a super-conservative game, because the blinds are becoming too big. So, you have to open up your game a bit, meaning that you need to take a few more risks.

Picking Your Spots

Taking a few more risks means picking spots when you can be the aggressor, when you can be the first one in the pot; that is, when you can do the pushing, not the calling. For example, if you're in a middle position, you might raise with the A♦ 10♦ or the K♣ J♣, whereas you may have passed with those hands earlier. Of course, if you get too much action, you have to pass. Actually, you might do the same types of things if you have doubled or tripled up and have one of the bigger stacks at the table. When everybody else is just hanging on, you're opening up because you have the chips to do it.

Playing a Short Stack

However, you don't want to open up too much if you're half-stacked, because you are more likely to get called or played with. You want to wait for a big pair or A-K, or play aggressively only in the last two seats when you have position. Short-stacked or not, if nobody has entered the pot and you're two spots away from the button, you're not going to throw away the A♦ 10♦. If you get raised, you can throw away your hand without committing all of your chips to it.

Short-stacked, I am going to move in all of my chips from fifth position on back with this type of hand if I have to—or at least put in enough chips to become committed to the pot. You're far less likely to get away from a hand short-stacked than if you have a bigger stack.

The point is that you have to take more risks with a short stack. You can't just wait around for aces or A-K because they aren't dealt to you often enough. You don't need to have a giant hand to start making some moves. Just be sure that you are the aggressor—that is, you are not reacting to your opponents, *they* are reacting to you.

The only time that this strategy doesn't run true is when you're playing against super-aggressive players who are sitting behind you, because they are liable to chop you off quickly. If you're playing with normal players, decent players, this is a very good strategy. But if you have an uber-aggressive player sitting behind you with a lot of chips, it doesn't work that well.

At this middle stage, more two or three-way pots will be played, whereas in the earlier stages there were a lot more multiway pots. There isn't nearly as much limping from the second round onward. The people who were playing any two suited cards in the earlier rounds have usually busted out of the tournament by the late middle stage.

LATE STAGE

At different stages in the tournament, you change your style of play from aggressive to semi-aggressive to passive. In the early stage, play solid poker. In the middle stage, you can play semi-aggressively, opening up your play in the right spots. Then in the late stage, when it gets down to three or four tables, you might need to play passively for a while. At a full table, you still play ring-game strategy. You want other players to knock each other out so that you can get to the final table.

Then you get to the "move" period when you're three or four places out of the money. This is when you play aggressive poker so that you can accumulate chips to be competitive at the money table. When you are two from the money, you can play very aggressively. However, if you're a couple of places out of the money with a short stack, you have a lot less maneuverability. You can't get too far out of line because somebody is going to look you up, hoping to bust you.

At this stage, aggressive players accumulate a lot chips by constantly keeping the heat on their opponents. With a medium or slightly above average stack, your opponents won't want to mess with you unless they have a real hand because it always takes greater strength to call a raise than to make a raise. In tournaments, you have to be very careful about the hands that you call raises with.

Move Times in Tournaments

All tournaments have certain "move" periods when you can pick up a lot of chips with bold play. One of them is when you are one table away from the pay table. At the World Series of Poker, which pays the final 10 percent of players, the move period is when you are approximately five to nine players from the published number of paid players.

For example, if 400 people signed up for the tournament, 40 players will get a payday. Suppose you look up at the tournament "clock," and notice that 47 players are still in action. You either see or sense that your table is tightening up to try to survive to the money. This is it, a move time when you can amass a great number of chips by opening up your play.

In the big events, when you first reach the pay tables, the payouts are a set amount for each player at the table. For example, in a 360-entry tournament that pays 10 percent of the field, each player who busts out in spots 36 through 28 will be paid the same amount. Then the payouts begin to increase with every diminishing position you are away from the final table. Eventually, the payouts begin rising according to the exact spot in which you finish—and that is when a lot of players really tighten their game. If you have the nerve, this period in a tournament gives you a great opportunity to amass a lot of chips.

Another move time is when you are two or three players away from the final table. Be aware that you have to know how to move—that is, open up your game—as well as when to execute against which players. You have to capitalize on your opponents' tight play. If you are willing to take a few extra risks, knowing that you might bust out and miss the big money, you have a chance at a massive reward. Even in today's very large tournament fields, the real money is still in the top three places.

BETTING YOURSELF OUT OF A POT

In pot-limit and no-limit tournaments and ring games, there are times when you might aggressively bet a drawing hand because you think you have a reasonable expectation of winning the pot. However, there are other times when you are far better off to just take a free card, especially when you are playing against tricky and aggressive players who do a lot of check-raising.

For example, suppose you have slipped into the pot from late position with A-8 suited and flop two to your suit:

YOU

FLOP

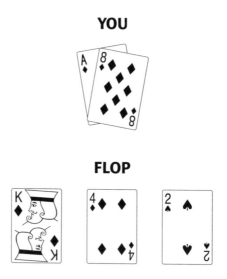

Three people in front of you are already in the pot, and two of them are tricky and aggressive. With this flop, you often would take a card off if somebody bets because you have an overcard working and the nut flush draw. But what if nobody bets on the flop? Against aggressive and tricky opponents, it is usually correct to also check and take the free card.

If you place a bet, especially if you make a pot-size bet, you will have to jeopardize too many of your chips to take the draw if somebody comes over the top of you with a maximum reraise. You are better off taking the free card and trying to hit your draw for nothing.

Now, let's look at a different scenario. You have the same A♦ 8♦ and the flop is the same, but you're up against only one opponent. Say that you have made a positional raise before the flop, the big blind called you, and now you are head-up. If he checks to you on the flop, you can bet the hand. Or say that, in addition to the big blind, there is one limper in the pot. They both are somewhat passive players. If they both check to you on the flop, you can bet.

Any time you think a bet will win the pot for you, go ahead and bet. Since a king is on the board, they may put you on a pair of kings rather than a flush draw. If neither of them has a king, it would be difficult for them to call your button bet. If one of them calls you with a little king, a K-7, for example, you can always check on the turn if you have no improvement, and wait for the river card to try to make your hand.

Of course, you could also make a second bet on the turn card if you think that a bet will win the pot for you, but that is a judgment call based on your knowledge of your opponents. There is always the danger that you could have made your hand cheaply, whereas you might get blown off the pot if you take an aggressive posture.

Remember than in pot-limit or no-limit, players can distort the size of the pot by putting in a significant bet, raise, or reraise. With a hand that you probably will make only one in three times, you will be paying too high a price if you have to put in a large amount of money to draw to it. This is why you have to be very selective when you have a drawing hand.

Some players play drawing hands too aggressively, rather than kicking back and playing them more passively.

What happens when you flop bottom two pair and are first to act? Suppose you are in the blind with 8-7, and the flop comes J-8-7.

YOU

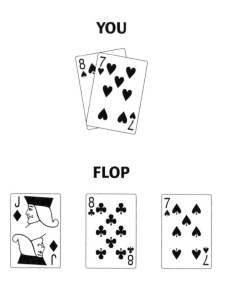

FLOP

How do you play your two pair?

Bottom two pair can be a dangerous hand. Say that you lead at the pot against several players and one of them comes over the top of you with a huge raise. He could have a straight, a set, or top two pair. It is better to check from the front and see what happens, rather than making a major commitment to the pot. If you had the same bottom two pair in last position, you might put in a bet if it is checked to you, taking the risk of being check-raised.

Now, say that you are in late position in an unraised pot with only two other people. Again, you have flopped bottom two pair. One of your opponents, an aggressive player who will represent hands that he doesn't have, bets in front of you. In this case, I might come over the top of him to protect my two pair.

Be leery of betting yourself off a hand that has some potential. If you can get a free card that may make the hand for you, the superior strategy usually is to take it. When you make a risky bet, you may open it up for someone to come over the top of you. Their raise may force you to fold when you could have had a free card that may have made your hand and gotten some action for you on the end.

THE LAST THREE TABLES

From the minute I sit down in a tournament, my goal is to make it to the top three payoff spots. It is never my goal to just get my money back. Actually, I'm only thinking of winning, but I will be satisfied to place in the top three because that's where the money is. But first, I have to move up from the third table to the final table.

By the time you get to the third table, you know your opponents. Your strategy is based on that knowledge and your chip count. The more chips you have, the more options and weapons at your disposal. If you are one of the shorter stacks, you realize you will be somewhat on the defensive since you don't have enough chips to intimidate your opponents. The bigger stacks are looking to bust you, and are sometimes willing to gamble with a slightly marginal hand to try to beat you. You are the bull's eye to them.

If you have an average stack or a big stack, it's a different ball game. An opponent has to have a hand to commit against you, unless he is extremely short-stacked and decides to take a stand. Or he might have a big stack and be willing to mix it up with anybody because he has a huge lead, though that is not a strategy we recommend.

Playing a Big Stack

When the top players have a lot of chips at the last three tables, they are not going to think, "I'm going to take a chance to bust this guy." Top players are not going to jeopardize their chips on a weaker hand. They want to get to the top three positions, so why should they give anybody a chance to double up at their expense? Top players will have a playable hand when they come into a pot; they're going to be the aggressor.

The old proverb in hold'em is, "A bettor or a raiser be; a caller never be." This is a very good guideline for this stage of play. If you're betting a pot, you could have the worst hand or the best hand, but you always have the chance to win because you bet. If you're calling, you have only one option: "Maybe I have this guy beaten."

The only time that you should be a caller past the flop in pot-limit or no-limit hold'em is when you are setting up an opponent, when you are laying a trap. Referring once again to the final table at the WSOP in 1993, Jim Bechtel had 6-6 against John Bonetti's A-K. A lot of players in Bechtel's spot would have raised preflop with the sixes, but Bechtel didn't. He played the hand to either catch a 6 or to throw it away. He figured Bonetti for a big hand and knew that if he caught a 6 on the flop, he could trap him for a lot of money. Of course, he caught the 6 on the flop.

Bechtel played the hand correctly, checking to trap an opponent, whereas a lesser player would either have moved in with the hand or would have thrown it away.

THE FINAL TABLE

Now it's nitty-gritty time, the time when you can win the tournament. To start with, you're playing in a full ring of nine players. In nine-handed play, you still want to try to play top hand all of the time. Of course, top hand doesn't have to be two aces; it could be two fives in certain situations. You play the best hand, whatever that best hand may be.

You will be playing basic strategy, except that you can sometimes pick up pots because the blinds are so big at this stage. However, you have to be very careful about when you try to steal. If you're the type of player who raises every time it's passed to you on the button, whether you have a hand or you have zilch, somebody is eventually going to chop you off.

Steal Situations

If you're going to try to steal a pot, you don't always need to be on the button. You can steal from the cutoff seat in front of the button or even two spots away from the button. I've done it from the first seat too. If you're raising from the first seat into eight other players, they're going to give you a lot of credit, especially if you have an image. Your opponents will need to have a pretty strong hand to call you, so you'll see them mucking hands such as A-J, A-Q, and K-Q suited.

If a front position player raises me, I might not necessarily muck my hand; it depends on what I know about his play. This is where that sixth sense that we've talked about comes into play, your feel for what's going on in the mind of the raiser. Is he capable of making a semibluff raise from up front? Most players are not capable of raising with a hand such as 9♥ 8♥, but a few of them are. Knowing who they are can make a difference in your bottom line.

Breaking Other Players

At the final table, remember that you don't have to break everybody at the table. Why not just wait and let them break each other? Sometimes when a player first starts playing tournaments, he will get to the last table in good chip position and, seeing that everybody is playing passively, take it upon himself to bust people. I think that we've probably all done that early in our careers. What often happens is that you bust several people out, then get to the final three, and finish in third place.

Analyzing his early career mistakes, Tom tells about the first final table he played: "I didn't slow down enough. I took risks against the short stacks, but of course, once you're in the top three, nobody is short-stacked. Then I got sawed off. I may have been better off by not knocking out as many people, by being a tad more selective or a tad less aggressive, by playing fewer hands.

"You see, you usually get a lot of respect by playing aggressively in short-handed play, but because I had been playing a ton of hands before the game got short-handed, my image had changed. My opponents didn't give me as much respect as they ordinarily would have given me, especially since they had seen me play a weak hand and bust out a player with it. Now they were more willing to mix it up with me, to go after me. So, it sometimes can work against you if your table image has changed during your play at the final table."

Tom and all the other top players, the champions of tournament poker, have taken the time to analyze their play all along their way to the top. They have plugged their leaks, erased their tells, and increased their paydays as the result of their continuing self examination.

THE FINAL FIVE

Now, suppose only five players are left in action. At this point, I'm going to get a little more aggressive. Of course, how aggressive I become depends on how many chips I have. If you have the command position in chips, people are always worried about messing with you because they know that you can break them. You can look around the table and see who is just trying to outlast the others.

For example, I was playing four-handed in a $500 tournament at the High Sierra and saw that two of the short stacks were trying to outlast each other just to survive and make it to the bigger money. They were playing "not to lose." I took advantage of them like Grant going through Richmond.

You can do the same thing in similar situations. Just keep chipping away at them, and since the blinds are so high, you're *really* chipping away because it's so expensive to play at that level.

Playing a Short Stack

If you're one of the short stacks with around five players left, you have to find a hand that you like and just go with it. You cannot let yourself get so short that the next time you have to post a blind, it will eat up all of your chips. If you let that happen, even if you double up, all you will have left is what you had before you were forced to post the blinds. Make your move *before* you get so short stacked that doubling up won't help you. This might mean moving in with virtually nothing.

I once played a tournament in which I had lost a couple of big pots. We were down to seven-handed play, the antes were $300 and the blinds were $1,000/$2,000. I had $8,000 in chips and it was costing me $5,100 a round to play. In the big blind, I held a 9-2 offsuit. The action was passed all the way around to the button, who held an A-J. He raised enough to move me all-in. My only hope in calling the raise and playing the hand was that I had live cards against an ace or a king. With five cards to come, I was only a 2 to 1 dog with any two live cards. I won the hand, and it wasn't too long before I had built my stack up to $70,000 in chips.

The key idea is that I didn't let myself get anteed and blinded down to the point that doubling up wouldn't have helped me. I'm not suggesting that you make this type of play, of course. But if you do, you have to know that the player on the button will raise without having a pair in his hand. If he's the type of player who only raises with pairs, you cannot make the call. When you are in the big blind, the only two raisers that you can call in a situation like this are the button and the little blind. You cannot call from a raise from an early position raiser.

You should always know *what* you are doing in a specific situation and *why* you are doing it. In this case, I made the call to try to avoid getting so short-chipped that even doubling up couldn't pull me out of the hole.

Chipping Away to Build Your Stack

Chipping away is a tournament tactic you can use to gain ground against your opponents. The idea is to defeat the other guy by bits and pieces. You can't be a fool when you chip away, you have to have the makings of a hand. You don't want to play a big pot unless you have a big hand. You want to start chipping away at players who have fewer chips than you, so that you keep building your stack as they're losing their stacks.

You begin to chip away at certain periods in the tournament, especially during the "move" times. Maybe I've noticed that they're raising with weak hands, so I go over the top of them. Stealing the blinds is another chipping away tactic that becomes important during "move" times. When you're close to getting into the money is one time when you can take advantage of every little situation by making moves that you probably haven't been doing very much of beforehand. This is the time to try some new things because, unless you run into a huge hand, you're going to get away with your chipping strategy over 90 percent of the time. It's well worth the risk.

Chipping Away in Heads-up Action

When I'm playing heads-up for all the marbles, I never play a pot that I don't raise—unless I'm limping in with a big pair. When you first start out, you test your opponent. The first couple of times, you flat call. If he raises every time you flat call, you put that in your memory bank. Then when you get a big hand, every once in a while you'll just flat call, and he'll do what he's been doing because that's the way most people play. You'll get him to commit a lot of chips when you get a big hand.

Realize that Q-7 is the average hand dealt. So if you can beat Q-7, you have a better than average hand heads-up. So you should raise if you can be the initial raiser. I'm not saying you should do this every time. You don't call raises with this kind of hand. And you don't call raises with a small ace unless you have a lot of chips than the other guy and you know he's desperate. In that case, you can probably raise with king high, queen high, or jack high.

But when you first start out and you're pretty close in chips, you can raise the man with A-5, but you don't want to call a raise with A-5. There's a big difference between raising with a hand and calling with that same hand. Player make a mistake in calling raises with weak aces when the chips are fairly even. That's a bad play.

Don't Let Them Breathe

You don't let the other guy breathe when you're chipping away at him. You just keep the pressure on him all the time in heads-up play. If you watched me playing Chris Ferguson at the final table in 2000, you saw me taking advantage of the pot every time I could. Actually, I played the most perfect poker I've ever played when we got to the final six that year. I felt that I never made one mistake at that table.

I only got my money in once with the worst hand before the flop, and that was in an 11 to 10 situation. That was when Hassan raised with 2-2 and I had the K♦ 10♦. We got it all in on that hand and I flopped a 10 to beat him. From my observations, I knew that he was likely to raise with a small pair or any two cards on the button. So, my play wasn't out of line. Other than that, I never made one mistake at that final table, which is unusual for me because we all usually make some mistakes along the line, and you lose some pots that way.

Chris had a huge 11 to 1 chip lead on me, so I just kept chipping away. I knew when he would bet a hand and I could put something to it; and I knew when he'd call a hand. I knew the whole works. I was in the zone.

On the final hand when I raised and he reraised and I moved him in, he got up, took off his hat and threw it on the ground, and walked around for several minutes before he put all his chips in. He said later that he knew he was beaten and that he had to get lucky because he couldn't beat me heads-up. I was thoroughly convinced that on that day, Chris had no chance of beating me heads-up unless he got lucky. He got lucky.

Winning the Main Event was one of the things I really wanted to do, because I'd won almost everything you could win and that's the one thing that had escaped me. And now the chances are very, very slim that any player can win the Big

One because you have to get through so many players. You have to get lucky and draw out on somebody once in a while, but you've also got to keep them from drawing out on you. It's tough, really tough, these days.

PLAYING HEADS-UP

In heads-up play, you are no longer concerned about chip count and you don't need as strong a starting hand to get involved with. Any ace is super-powerful. Pocket pairs, eights and higher, also are strong, but small pocket pairs, the deuces through the sevens, are not nearly as strong as they are in other heads-up situations. This is true because players will call you with hands like J-10 and 9-8 knowing they are only 11 to 10 dogs.

You might play the lower pairs, but you shouldn't commit all your money with them before the flop. If your opponent has two paints in his hand, he will probably call a raise. The all-powerful card in heads-up play is the ace.

Any time you're playing heads-up with an opponent who has a 3 to 1 chip lead over you, remember that you are still only two all-in hands away from winning the tournament. And sometimes when you're playing heads-up, you move into a "zone" that feels something like the great marathon runners talk about.

For example, at the Diamond Jim Brady $10,000 buy-in no-limit hold'em tournament at the Bicycle Casino, I had $120,000 and Tuna Lund had $360,000. I was chipping away at him, meaning that I was winning every pot from him by being super-aggressive. In fact, I won fourteen out of fifteen hands, a little bit here and a little bit there. When we got to the point where he was only 2 to 1 in chips against me, Tuna asked if I wanted to make a deal. I said no, and we continued to play.

I had been chipping away at him so intensively that I knew he was going to run a bluff on me. It had gotten to the stage where he had to do something to try to take the aggressive position away from me. Then a hand came up in which a J-9-4 came on the flop. I'm known for playing J-9, "my hand" when it's suited in clubs, but this time I only had a 9. Tuna bet the flop and I raised him just a little bit. Then off came a 3. He took the lead with a $40,000 bet, and I thought to myself, "I know I've got him, even though I only have second pair."

I called the $40,000, and thought that if neither a king nor an ace came on the river, he was going to bluff at the pot. The board paired threes on the end, which was perfect for my hand. Tuna bet $50,000 and I called.

"Before you turn your hand over," I told him, "let me tell you what you have. You have a Q-10 offsuit." He turned his hand over and there it was, the Q-10. Just as I thought, he had picked up a draw to the J-9, and as I predicted, when he didn't hit it, he bluffed at me on the river. Suddenly, I had the lead in the tournament. A few hands later, I raised with two tens, he moved all-in with two eights, and it was all over.

The year before that at the Diamond Jim Brady tournament, Mansour Matloubi, the 1990 World Champion of Poker, and I were playing heads-up for the championship. I had the Jh 7h in my hand and he had two hearts in his hand. The board came with two hearts and a 7. I led at the pot and he called. A rag came on fourth street, he checked to me, I bet, and he called.

On the end, the board showed three overcards to my 7. Mansour had not run a bluff for five hours of play at the final table—but he went all-in with his last $120,000 on the river. I beat him into the pot with fourth-best pair.

"You've got me," he said. "I'm bluffing."

The Zone

Heads-up is a whole different ball game. You can make these types of moves based on your observation, your feel for the game, and your opponents. When you're in your zone, your opponent recognizes that and he has to make a move to get you out of your cycle. To this day, Mansour laughs about my calling him with those two sevens, saying that it was the greatest play he's ever seen in hold'em. Of course, the call wouldn't have busted me, but that didn't enter into my decision. I was in the zone, and when you're there, you have "balls of iron," you *know* when you have the best hand.

You have to have the courage of your convictions in spots like this, when you have a dead read on your opponent. Many times, a lesser player will have the same read, but won't have the courage to act on his convictions. He takes the easy way out and mucks his hand.

The third time I won the Diamond Jim Brady, I was at the final table with Eskimo Clark, Hal Kant and Bobby Hoff, who was short-stacked. I brought it in, Hal folded, Eskimo raised it, and Bobby moved in his short stack.

"Well, I know that Eskimo has some kind of a king-hand, judging from the way he has been raising four-handed," I thought. "I have A-J and a whole lot of chips, so I'm gonna move over the top of Bobby and shut Eskimo out to get head-up with Bobby."

And that's exactly the move that I made. Eskimo folded his K-Q, and Bobby and I ended up splitting the pot—we both had an A-J. To Eskimo's chagrin, the board came K-Q and to this day, he still talks about having the best hand. But before the flop, he didn't have top hand and I shut him out so that he couldn't win the pot. These are the types of plays that come from experience and from the feel that you develop for certain situations.

TOURNAMENT ACTION HANDS

This chapter is designed to show you how to put knowledge into action on the green felt, whether it's the real stuff in a big Las Vegas tournament, or the virtual felt on the screen in an online event. In particular, we picture hands and situations in which you've been dealt pocket aces and pocket kings, the two biggest hands in hold'em, plus a few other types of hands you might typically play. We deal you the same hand more than once, and change the situation to demonstrate how your position, the actions of your opponents, and other crucial factors influence your strategy for playing the hand.

TOURNAMENT ACTION HAND 1

A-A in Early Position

Let's look at several situations that demonstrate how you might play pocket aces from early position when you are the first player in the pot.

Situation One

You are Player A sitting in early position and have been dealt:

YOU

You limp into the pot. The player next to the button raises. The button and both of the blinds fold. You decide to just call. The flop comes:

FLOP

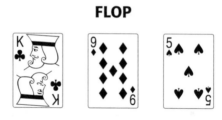

Now what do you do? Since you have set things up to slow-play your hand, you check. Player B bets. What's your play? You just flat call.

Now, suppose the turn card is the 2♠:

TURN

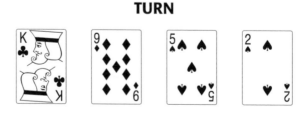

You check. Player B puts in a big bet. What do you do?

You raise, knowing that there's a good chance that you'll get played with if Player B has something like A-K or a pocket pair such as queens or jacks. Player B calls. The river card is another deuce:

RIVER

You bet. Player B calls and shows A♠ K♠. He had top pair with the nut flush draw on the turn.

Action Analysis

Because you limped, he probably thought that he had the best hand by a long shot, or at the worst, a tie. He didn't put you on a set, and most players wouldn't even consider that you might have two aces. This is the perfect situation for slow-playing pocket aces and getting full value from them. It is one way of trapping your opponent.

Now let's look at a different way to slow-play aces from early position.

Situation Two

You are sitting in early position with:

YOU

This time you raise from with your pocket aces. Player B reraises. What do you do? You flat call.

The board comes the same as Situation One.

FLOP

What do you do? Lead at the pot with a standard bet.

Action Analysis

When the flop comes K-9-5, you are thinking, "How can I get the most out of this pot? If I lead, Player B probably will raise if he has A-K." You lead at the pot with a standard bet—you don't want him to fold, so you don't make a huge bet. You want to bet the amount that you believe he will call if he has any kind of hand.

Whether he calls or raises, you have him trapped—unless, of course, he has pocket kings, in which case you're the one who is trapped. You lead at this hand all the way through—his preflop reraise and call on the flop tell you that he is pot-committed. In this situation, your preflop raise built a decent pot for you to win.

Situation Three

You raise from early position with:

YOU

Player B reraises. Player C cold-calls the reraise. Now what do you do?

Bet all in.

Action Analysis

In this situation, you know that Player C has a big hand, probably K-K or Q-Q, so you go over the top with an all-in bet. There's plenty of money in the pot already, so you simply move on it. You hope for a call, but even if neither Player B nor Player C calls, you still have won a decent pot.

Situation Four

Now suppose the action happens like this:

YOU

You raise from early position. Player B reraises. Player C cold-calls the reraise. But this time, you reraise, Player B folds, and Player C calls your reraise.

The flop comes the same as before:

FLOP

How do you play the hand?

You have two options: You either lead at it all the way, or you just move in on the flop. You want to get paid off on your aces, but even if Player C does not call, you've still won a big pot with your aggressive play of pocket aces from up front.

TOURNAMENT ACTION HAND 2

A-A in Middle Position

Now let's investigate some ways to play aces from a middle position.

Situation One

You are sitting in a middle position with:

Suppose you're in a real action game, Player A just calls, you just call, two or three other players also limp, and then Action Al, who has been raising every pot, puts in a raise. What do you do?

Whenever the pot is opened or raised in the first three seats, you have two options:

(1) You can reraise, or
(2) You can play second-hand low

In this situation, you have set things up to play second-hand low. You know that Action Al is sitting behind you, so when somebody leads into the pot in front of you, you just call. You suspect that the original limper might also have a big hand, so you're setting the stage to raise both the limper and the action player.

Action Analysis

The first player in the pot might have a decent hand, but you have the best hand you can be dealt in hold'em. Player A or Action Al might reraise the pot and if so, you will have a big pot to win before the flop. So if you reraise right there, they might figure that you're just trying to pick up the pot, or that you have an A-K or something like that. They hardly ever put you on aces when you play second-hand low. You're trying to trap everybody. You want to make them pay to try to draw out on your aces.

Now let's take a look at another situation when you're holding aces in a middle position.

Situation Two

Again you are in middle position holding:

YOU

You raised the pot before the flop. Player B called on the button and Player C called in the big blind.

The flop comes:

FLOP

You make a standard bet in the hope of getting called by an A-Q, K-Q, Q-J, Q-10, a 9 with a big kicker, a J-10 (straight draw), or even someone with a diamond draw. You could get beaten by these drawing hands or by the pair hands if they double-pair with their kicker. But in all of these situations, you still are the favorite on the flop.

The only drawing hand you could face that is favored over your aces is the J♦ 10♦, and even that hand is only slightly favored.

The fourth street card is the 5♥.

TURN

On the turn, be sure to bet enough to put pressure on your opponents. You want to force them to make a decision as to whether they want to commit a lot of money to this pot. Obviously you are a good favorite over all the hands that we have mentioned.

The 2♥ comes on the river.

RIVER

If anyone has stayed in the hand with you to the river, I would empty out (bet all my chips) hoping to get called. The way that the hand has been played should indicate that A-A is still the best hand.

Action Analysis

In this situation, I did not forget about the possibility that an opponent might have flopped a set. But because of the straight and flush possibilities on board, I am sure that if anyone had flopped a set, he would have moved on the flop, or certainly on fourth street.

Situation Three

Before the flop, one player limps in from an early position. You know from his previous play that he could be holding anything. You are the next to act. Your hand is:

YOU

You decide to just call. The button, the small blind and the big blind also flat call.

FLOP

The two blinds and the early limper check.What do you do?

You also check. The button bets, the two blinds fold, and the original limper calls. Obviously you don't know exactly what hands the button and the limper have, but you do know that you have the best possible hand now. Therefore you have two choices:

(a) Flat call. You have disguised the strength of your hand in the hope of winning a huge pot on fourth or fifth street.

(b) Raise the pot on the flop. You don't want to give any free cards.

Let's take a look at two possible scenarios that illustrate these two options.

Choice A: Flat Call on the Flop

Along with the early-position limper, you flat called the button's bet on the flop. The turn card is the 10♣.

TURN

Now you have them where you want them, but how do you get the most value from your hand? If the limper checks, lead at the pot with a decent bet in the hope of either getting raised and/or called by either or both of your opponents. Then if either player raises, he has committed himself to the pot. In that case, go on the offensive and move all in. You know that there is a very good chance that at least one of them is on a big draw, has flopped a set, or has top two pair.

Now, suppose one of them calls your all-in bet and the river comes:

RIVER

You're in clover!

But what if either or both opponents just flat call on the turn? In that case, on fifth street when you know that you have the nuts, bet an amount that you think they will call. Don't move in because you don't want them to throw their hands away—you simply want to get full value from your aces.

The difference between good players and average players is that a good player always does whatever it takes to get full value from a hand.

Choice B: Raise on the Flop

Now suppose you choose to raise the pot right on the flop so as not to give any free cards, but still with the hope that either or both opponents will call your raise. Understand that if either opponent calls the raise, his hand would have to be a set, top two pair, top and bottom pair, A-K or A-Q, a flush draw, or a pair with a flush draw. In this case, if someone has a pair and a flush draw, he would have to have an ace and a flush draw.

Let's say that both the limper and the button call your raise. Again, the board looks like this on fourth street:

TURN

The limper checks. What do you do?

You make a big bet, in the hope of either winning the pot right there or getting called by either or both opponents.

Suppose the button calls and the limper folds. Again the 5♠ comes at the river.

RIVER

This time you are the first to act—what do you do?

It's time for the kill! You've put him on a big hand, so you shove in all your chips to find out just how important his hand is to him. Does life get much sweeter than this?

TOURNAMENT ACTION HAND 3

A-A in Late Position

Playing pocket aces in late position is easier than playing them from any other spot.

The Situation

Suppose you are sitting in late position with:

YOU

How do you play your hand?

Raise. It doesn't matter how many people are in the pot, you're going to raise. If a lot of players are in the pot and someone has raised in front of you, you're going to reraise. You cannot give free cards very often in a tournament if you want to survive. A lot of times too, your opponents will discount the strength of a late-position raise and will play with you because they believe you're on a steal.

Action Analysis

After everyone has passed to the button, you sometimes will see people limp with pocket aces, but I think that's a horrible play. The chances of someone raising from either of the two blinds are slim since you have two of the four aces in the deck locked up. And if they don't raise, they're going to get free cards on the flop with any kind of hand. Then you will have no idea about where you are with your aces. This is why

I think that you definitely should raise with aces when you're in late position.

Make your standard raise if you're the first one in the pot, or if only one player has limped in front of you. But if more than one player already is in the pot, you should consider moving all in. Any time you have pocket aces, you want someone to come after you with a reraise.

If an opponent reraises, your decision is whether to just flat call and try to nail him after the flop, or move in immediately to try to win the pot right there. If you flat call, there's always the danger that your opponent will outflop you. Of course, when you're playing aces in no-limit poker, you always try to maximize your hand, so you choose the strategy that will best serve that purpose.

TOURNAMENT ACTION HAND 4

A-A in the Blind

Playing any hand from the blinds is trickier than playing from any other position because you are out of position in the betting sequence from the flop to the river.

The Situation

Suppose you are sitting in the small blind holding:

YOU

How do you play your hand?

Raise. When you have aces in one of the blinds, it is more important to raise than it is from any other position. Why? Because after the flop, you always have to act first. You're in the weakest position at the start of the hand, so you need to play aces like you're supposed to play them—raise.

Now suppose everybody checks to the button. The button raises and the small blind folds. What do you do?

In this situation you might try to trap him by just flat calling the raise in the hope that something will come on the flop that hits him a little bit, but hits you even better. The best situation that you could hope for is that your opponent has something like A-6.

TOURNAMENT ACTION HAND 5

K-K in a Tournament

Getting dealt kings, the second-best hand in hold'em, is always good news in tournaments. But, they're more difficult to play correctly than you might think. The reason K-K is so hard to play is because it seems that an ace so often comes on the flop when you have kings in the hole.

Situation One

You are playing in the middle stage of a $1,000 buy-in no-limit hold'em tournament. You are the first to act. You have been dealt:

YOU

How would you play the hand before the flop?

You might limp with the two kings from front position, hoping that someone will raise. If somebody behind you has pocket aces, the more power to him. If you run into aces, there's nothing you can do about it.

The strategy behind limping with the kings is to let somebody raise so that you can reraise and win the pot right there. If a player just calls, you still have the second-best hand that you can start with, and you're just hoping that no ace comes on the board.

Situation Two

Say that you limp with the kings, Player B raises, and Player C calls the raise. Now what? You reraise. More than likely, you will win the pot right there, unless either Player B or C has aces or queens.

If either one of them reraises you, you're probably a gone goose. If Player B has aces, for example, he will move you all-in. If he doesn't do that, there's a pretty good chance that you have the best hand. If Player C reraises, he would have to be a very good player to be playing second hand low.

Recall that when someone plays second hand low, he just calls with a big hand (in this case, A-A) in the hope that somebody behind him will raise and drive the first bettor back into him so that he can get all the money in before the flop. It takes a very good player to pull off this play, and you don't see it very often in tournaments; it is used more frequently in cash games. Therefore, it is unlikely that Player C is using this strategy.

Action Analysis

Two kings is the second-best pair you can be dealt, but it also is the most dangerous. Why? Because it is a very hard hand to get away from before the flop. Usually, if there is one raise, you're going to reraise with two kings. Of course, you might run into two aces, or a big ace, or even "any ace." If somebody with an ace in his hand calls you, you're a goner if an ace comes on the flop, no matter how strong an ace he's holding.

Any time the flop has been raised and reraised before it gets to you in a tournament, I suggest that you dump your two kings. Even if you are wrong once in a while, you will save a lot of money in the long run.

TOURNAMENT ACTION HAND 6

K-K Early in a Big Tournament

Now, let's take a look at a hand that came up during the first level of play at the $10,000 Main Event at the World Series of Poker a few years ago. I picked up these cards:

T.J.

I made it $300 to go. Jay Heimowitz, who is an expert player, called. Here came the flop:

FLOP

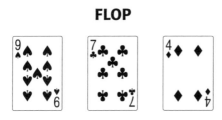

I bet $400 at the pot and Jay made a big raise of around $3,000. I didn't hesitate in throwing away the kings.

Why? Because I knew that he wouldn't be raising me with anything less than two aces or a set. Sure enough, he showed me pocket nines. Because of the caliber of player Jay is, I knew that he would not have stood a raise with a hand such as A-J, so he must have had a pocket pair. The only pairs that I could have beaten on the flop were tens, jacks, or queens. When you're playing against a top player like Jay, he isn't moving in with two jacks, two queens, or even two kings.

I figured that he either had two aces or a set. He wouldn't have 10-8 or 8-6 for a straight draw. I lost $700 on the hand, but at least I wasn't knocked out.

Actually, this was the second time in a row that Jay had flopped top set against an overpair. On the hand that came up just before this one, Tommy Grimes had A-A and brought it in for about $400, the standard raise. Jay called the bet. The flop came 10-7-2. Tommy bet $2,000 at the pot and Jay moved in. Tommy made the mistake of calling him. Jay had 10-10, flopped top set, and knocked Tommy out of the tournament. At least I had spared myself that agony by folding to Jay's big raise.

Action Analysis

How you play pocket kings against a rag flop depends, once again, on what you know about your opponents. If I were playing Joe Blow from Idaho, I might give him a little action on this hand, especially if I knew that he was a former limit hold'em player. Limit players seem to think they have the Holy City when they have top pair with top kicker, or an overpair, in no-limit hold'em.

A world-class player like Jay knows that I either have an overpair or am taking a shot with A-K or A-Q (since it was a small flop). He also knows that I am putting him on either A-K or A-Q too. But once I bet the flop and he raised it, I knew where he was with the hand.

Why did he make such a huge raise? If he put me on a big overpair, he may have figured that I would play it, but I fooled him and didn't fall into that trap. He also knew that if he flat called, I would shut down if I didn't hit anything, so he figured that he may as well try to get me to play the hand on the flop. Also, of course, he didn't want to give a free card in tournament play.

Jay knew that he had the pot won on the flop, so why not take it right then? Why give me a chance to bust him if one of my cards came off on the turn? Hence, the big raise on the flop.

TOURNAMENT ACTION HAND 7

K-K in the Middle Stage of a Tournament

You are holding two kings in the middle stage of a $1,000 tournament.

YOU

You raised before the flop and Player A called. The flop comes:

FLOP

Situation One

Player A checks. What do you do?

A lot of players will check the ace on the flop. You also check.

Situation Two

This time you are sitting in first position with the kings. The flop is the same as above. What do you do?

You check because the ace is on the board. Player B probably also checks. A good player will check his ace on the flop if the raiser has checked in front of him.

Now, suppose the turn comes with the 2♣.

TURN

What's your move?

In a tournament, you check again. Player B probably will bet on the turn, although he may delay betting until fifth street. He knows that you don't have an ace and he may try to trap you on the end.

When an ace comes on the flop, you are through with the hand and will only play it for a showdown.

TOURNAMENT ACTION HAND 8

K-K in the Middle Stage Again

Amazingly, you are dealt two kings for the third time during the middle stage of the tournament. You raised before the flop and two players called. This time, you are determined to win with your cowboys.

YOU

FLOP

The Situation

You lead with the kings in the hope that an opponent holds a hand such as A♠ Q♦ or K♥ Q♥, which are hands that someone might call a raise with. If one of those hands is out, then you might get a play when you bet. Suppose the 6♥ comes on the turn.

TURN

What's your best play at this point?

Make a good-sized bet. You don't want to give anybody a chance to make two pair.

Action Analysis

There's always the chance that you're up against a player who stood your preflop raise with Q-Q. Some tournament players think that queens are the holy nuts and will even reraise with them. However, since nobody reraised before the flop, you go with the kings and then try to shut them out on fourth street with a big bet.

There is also the chance that someone holds a K-J suited and will call your opening bet on a straight draw. Although he will probably call you on the flop, if you put in a big bet at fourth street, he will throw away the hand—unless he is a horrible player, that is. In no-limit or pot-limit hold'em, you can freeze out the draws on the turn, whereas in limit hold'em you cannot do that.

TOURNAMENT ACTION HAND 9

K-K at the World Series of Poker

This hand came up at the WSOP when Hans "Tuna" Lund and I were involved in a hand.

Here are our hands:

T.J.	**TUNA**

The Situation

Tuna raised the pot from early position and it was passed all the way to me on the button.

I flat called him with my pocket kings. The flop came:

FLOP

What would you do?

I flat called the bet. When a blank came on the turn, he led at the pot again. This time, I moved over the top of him. He folded his hand, and I raked in the pot.

Action Analysis

It isn't wrong to take a chance once in a while. You hear so many people say, "Every time I have kings, an ace comes on the flop." If an ace comes, so what? Just throw away the hand. In this example, I played to win a big pot, and was able to extricate $2,700 from my opponent. I knew that Tuna was likely to be holding A-Q or A-K before the flop, but there was a pretty good chance that I held the best hand, even though kings is the second-best pair you can be dealt.

In limit, pot-limit, and no-limit hold'em tournaments, it is not unusual for players to raise from early position with an A-Q. I don't suggest raising with it in a full ring, but five-handed or less, I will raise with the hand.

At a full table, I think that hands such as A-Q, A-J, or A-10 (suited or unsuited) in the first four seats should be played like you'd play 2-3. Why? Because if you stand a raise with them, you're putting yourself in kicker trouble if an ace comes on the flop. It seems that when you start with the worst hand, you invariably flop a pair to it and then you're stuck in the pot. You try to avoid that situation by not playing these types of hands in early position, especially in a no-limit hold'em tournament.

TOURNAMENT ACTION HAND 10

J-J in the Early Stage of a Tournament

A pocket pair of jacks can be a tricky hand to play in tournament action. The later your position at the table, the easier pocket jacks are to play. Let's start with an early-position scenario and progress from there.

Situation One

You are sitting in early position, the first three or four seats, in the early stage of a no-limit hold'em tournament. You have been dealt:

YOU

Do you bring it in with a raise before the flop, or do you just limp in?

You limp with J-J or 10-10 in this situation. If you raise and get reraised, what are you going to do with the hand? If you don't get raised, you could flop a jack and win a big pot, because nobody will put you on that big a hand to start with. By not raising preflop, you take the chance that an opponent will come into the pot with something like a little ace or K-Q and beat you. If someone outflops you, you would have been beaten anyway. However, by not raising before the flop, you will lose less money if you get beaten.

Of course, if you had raised before the flop, they may not have played those little-ace or K-Q hands. But you have a bigger worry than that preflop: Getting reraised and being forced to throw away the hand when you have money invested in the pot.

Situation Two

You are sitting in fifth position, right in the middle of the pack, and everyone has passed to you. Now how do you play your jacks?

I would raise with the jacks whether or not it is early in the tournament. There is a big difference between these two situations. In this situation, four people are already out of the pot and there are only four players sitting behind you.

Early in a big buy-in tournament when the antes are $25/$50, you might raise $150 to $200 with the jacks. In a big buy-in tournament, you may still have $10,000 in front of you, so $200 would be a reasonable raise. You don't make a huge raise of, say, $4,000 early in a tournament. You make the small raise because you think that you have the best hand before the flop.

You are trying to do one of two things: either win the pot right there; or get called and win the pot as it develops. Pocket jacks aren't the best starting hand that you can have, and you can't even call with them on a lot of flops.

Situation Three

You are in the late stages of a tournament with the two jacks in your hand. How do you play them? Later in the tournament, you definitely want to raise with the two jacks.

Say that you are playing at a short-handed table with six or fewer players. Four tables are left in the tournament and each one of them is short-handed. In this case, you want to play the jacks much stronger than you would have played them earlier, although you don't necessarily want to commit your whole stack with them.

TOURNAMENT ACTION HAND 11

Ace-Wheel Card in Middle Position

Ace-wheel card falls into the category of "any ace," a hand with an ace in it and a low kicker. These types of hands can put you in a world of worry.

In order to play an ace with a wheel card profitably, the right set of circumstances should be in place. Ace-little suited or unsuited is not a hand that you should play from an early position. It is of little value to you from up front because if an ace comes on the flop and you bet it and get played with, you have no kicker.

Obviously the best flop for ace-small suited is three to your suit or three wheel cards. But the odds are so great against getting that ideal flop that if you play ace-small every time you get it, you will be a big loser to the hand.

The Situation

You have been dealt:

YOU

You are in middle to late position and a couple of player have limped into the pot. Should you fold, call or raise?

Since it is developing into a multiway pot, you might limp with ace-small and see the flop cheaply. If you get a good flop to it in multiway action, you have the chance to win a nice pot.

You don't want to stand a raise with A-4 and you don't want to play it heads-up. Therefore, when you call a limp bet, be prepared to throw your hand away if someone raises. Folding against a raise should be a part of your thinking even before you limp into the pot.

TOURNAMENT ACTION HAND 12

Ace-Wheel Card in Late Position

Can you ever play ace-small from the last two positions? Yes, if no one else has entered the pot. But you don't raise with it, you limp.

The Situation

Suppose you're in the cutoff seat or on the button and no one has entered the pot. You have been dealt ace-small.

YOU

Should you raise with ace-small to try to bully the blinds?

No. You don't want to put yourself in a situation where you cannot get rid of this type of hand before the flop. Personally,

I never play this hand strongly. In no-limit circles we call it a sucker hand.

Let's say that you couldn't resist raising on the button with the hand, and the small blind calls your raise. What could he have? He probably has an ace in his hand or a pocket pair. And almost any kicker that he has with his ace will be higher than your wheel card. Even if his kicker also is a wheel card, you still are not a favorite to the hand most of the time if an ace falls.

As I have maintained for years, if the four or five players in front of you don't have a hand, there's a good chance that one or two of the players behind you do have one. That is why you limp rather than raise with ace-small in late position—you cannot stand a reraise, you have to release it. And if you raise and get called, you don't have a hand. If you want to go further with it, you have to be prepared to bluff with the hand unless you catch a flop to it. Why put yourself in that kind of situation? Your goal is to always be in control.

TOURNAMENT ACTION HAND 13

Ace-Small in the Small Blind

When you are in the small blind against the big blind only with an ace-small, you have three options: raise, fold or call. If you just call, you might get yourself into trouble. If you fold, you stay out of trouble. If you raise, you might win the pot right there. It depends on how you feel about it.

YOU

If you have observed that your opponent usually defends his blind, forget about raising. Consider limping against this type of opponent.

If he is someone who raises all the time, he might raise just because you limped. Sometimes, depending on the type of player he is, you can reraise him. Other times, against a different player, fold if he raises. What you decide to do depends on the kind of read you put on your opponent.

What about playing hands like A-6, A-7, or A-8? Whether you're the small blind, the big blind, in the front, middle or late position, you're just throwing your money away if you play these types of hands—except in very selective situations (heads-up, for example). None of these ace-middle-card hands can make a straight. Your best result is the nut flush if the hand is suited, or two pair if you hit your kicker.

TOURNAMENT ACTION HAND 14

Ace-Wheel Card in a Major Tournament

This hand came up at the 2002 Hall of Fame no-limit hold'em tournament. Howard Lederer and Peter Costa were playing heads-up at the final table for the title, the gold watch, and the money. Howard held A♦ 4♦. Peter had K-6 offsuit.

HOWARD

PETER

The flop came:

FLOP

Costa bet $30,000 and Lederer raised all-in. "I can't find a reason to lay the hand down," Costa said. He called the raise.

The turn and river brought Lederer no help with either a diamond or an ace. Costa won the title. Cruel things can happen when you play these small-ace hands, even when you're heads-up, have the best hand going in, and catch a draw to the nut flush with the best overcard in the world. Howard certainly was correct in playing the hand strong, especially when Peter had him outchipped, but Lady Luck was not on his side.

TOURNAMENT ACTION HAND 15

Another Ace-Wheel Card Situation in a Major Tournament

At the Four Queens Classic in 1996, Doyle Brunson and I were playing heads-up for the title in the $5,000 no-limit hold'em event. I looked down at the A♠ 2♠. Doyle had J-9 offsuit.

T.J.	DOYLE

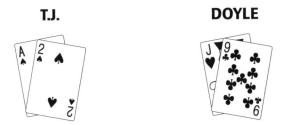

I raised a significant amount before the flop. Doyle called my big raise. The flop came:

FLOP

Doyle was the first to act and he bet into me with his bottom two pair, jacks and nines. I had flopped the top pair *and* the nut flush draw, so I moved all in on him. Doyle called.

On the river the board looked like this:

RIVER

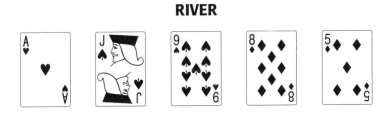

When the 8♦ came on the turn and the 5♦ came on the river, my big pair with a big draw bit the dust, just like Howard at the Hall of Fame. Doyle's two pair stood up like iron to win the pot and the championship.

This hand just proves once again that the luck factor comes into play in all of poker. You might make the right play with the best hand, you might do it in the perfect situation, but nothing you do guarantees that you're going to get the right results.

Just ask me!

HOW TO WIN BIG BY PLAYING SMALL EVENTS & SATELLITES

There are two major ways to practice for the big no-limit tournaments: Play in the small tournaments, the $200 and $300 buy-in events, and play the one-table satellites for the big tournaments. Although you don't get as many chips to start with as you do in the World Series of Poker events, playing in smaller tournaments is a good way to learn how to play tournament poker.

Just remember that you usually are playing against people who are on your same skill level, or possibly just a bit above you; but you seldom are playing the top players. Because you can beat someone at your level of skill doesn't mean that you are a world-beater. You have to be able to beat the people on the top level.

A lot of cardrooms sponsor small buy-in no-limit tournaments where you can win a seat for the WSOP $10,000 main event. I suggest that you play in these tournaments to get experience in playing the World Series structure, in which you have a lot of chips to start with. I use exactly the same method of play in $500 tournaments that I do in $5,000 or $10,000 tournaments. The element that makes the WSOP's final event so different from the lesser buy-in tournaments is that you start with $10,000 in chips. Obviously, more play is possible when you begin with $10,000 chips than when you start with only $500 in chips. The experience that you will get from these events is far superior to playing satellites, though satellites also have a role to play in preparing yourself to play in major tournaments.

ONE-TABLE SATELLITES

A lot of the best players use the one-tables to make extra money, so they are a good place to get experience playing against top players. In the one-table satellites for a big tournament, you can learn a lot about how players play and how they treat situations. And you also have enough chips to maneuver around and play the game.

The entry fee for the $5,000 one-table satellites is $500; for the $10,000 big one, it is $1,000. Although that's a lot of money to pay for a satellite, you can learn a lot and end up making plenty of money in the long run. One thing that I like about the one-table satellites for the WSOP Main Event is that you get $2,000 in chips, which gives you some maneuverability. In the one-table satellites for the $5,000 and $10,000 tournaments, you have more chips to start with, and the blinds start out smaller in relation to the size of the chips in play. Also, the rounds are twenty minutes (rather than fifteen minutes), giving more advantage to the better players. In a one-table satellite, you play down to the final winner, unless you make a deal on the end.

MEGASATELLITES

The megasatellites, in which you get $200 in chips, are much tougher to win because they become move-in games. This is why I don't think that megasatellites are as good a learning experience as the one-tables or the smaller tournaments. But don't get me wrong: I'm all for megasatellites. Winning one of them may be the only way that some people have of getting into the big tournaments. In fact, a great many players win their entries into the WSOP in the megasatellites.

The WSOP issues a lammer, a chip equivalent to the buy-in for the big tournament you were playing for. You may use that lammer for a tournament entry of the equivalent cash value, or trade it in for cash.

Remember, too, that you don't have to *win* a megasatellite to get a seat in the big tournament. Several seats for the Main Event usually are given out at each of the big satellites, so you only need to place among the top finalists. As soon as the satellite is played down to a certain number of people, seats are awarded and the game is over.

The purpose of playing satellites is to get into a tournament cheaply, not to learn how to play tournament poker, although a lot of people like to play the megasatellites so that they can get experience playing against top players. Satellites for big tournaments also can be a very good way of making pocket cash.

One year at the Hall of Fame tournament, I played in six megasatellites and won a seat in four of them. Then I played in six one-table satellites and also won a seat in four of those, so the satellites turned out to be profitable ventures for me.

YOUR BEST VALUE

More money is given away in tournaments than anybody ever thought of giving away in side games. This is the main reason why your best value in a tournament is the tournament itself, not the side games, especially at World Series time.

A lot of weak players enter WSOP events, either by winning a satellite or by ponying up $2,000 and more. Good players have a huge overlay, especially in pot-limit and no-limit games, because the skill factor is so much higher in these games than it is in limit hold'em. For example, when 145 people signed up for the final event in 1985, we looked over the list of players and said, "Well, there are seventy-five who have no chance at all; there might be thirty-five players who can go all the way to the third day; there are about twenty-five who can make the final table; and maybe ten of those twenty-five actually could win it."

All of the top players like having larger fields, because a lot of people who are capable of winning a satellite seldom win a major tournament. Why? Because they are not able to put their game together for two to four days. They may play very well during the first day, but they cannot do it over the long haul because their skill level just isn't high enough.

SATELLITE STRATEGY

I have heard a lot of people suggest that playing satellites is a good way for limit hold'em players to learn how to play no-limit. I think that is a fallacy. In a satellite, you begin with very few chips. If you're playing in a $10,000 or $5,000 satellite, you start with only $200 to $500 in chips. With so few chips, it is basically a move-in game with all the play taken out of it. Because the antes go up every fifteen minutes or so, you usually move your chips all in when you get a hand that you like, whereas in a ring game, you try to use your abilities and play out a pot.

At the Golden Nugget, I once played in a $10,000 satellite in which five people moved in their entire stacks ($2,000) on the first hand. So, after the very first hand, one player had $10,000 and nobody else had more than $2,000. But guess what? He didn't win it! In fact, he didn't even come in second.

The way to play satellites is to sit back and let the other players knock each other out. Wait for a big hand. You get $300 in chips in a no-limit $500 satellite. The beginning blinds are $5/$15 with no ante. In a ten-handed game, it costs you $20 every round (every ten hands) for the first fifteen minutes. Then the blinds rise to $10/$25, so every round costs you $40 during the next fifteen minutes.

During the first half hour, you should be able to pick up at least one hand. A lot of people play 8-6, A-7 (any ace), K-Q, or any two suited cards, and they get busted with those types of hands. By waiting patiently for a hand, you may suddenly find yourself down to four-handed play, and you don't have many chips.

A lot of players panic at this point because they are short-stacked and the other players have a lot of chips. But the blind structure remains the same, so you can pick up a couple of hands and get back in the ball game if you play correctly. This is why I believe that the way to play satellites is to let players knock out each other and then you take on the survivors. You get dealt a good hand, win it to get back into the ball game, and then you simply outplay them. You start attacking them when it gets down to three or four players. I have won a lot of satellites using this strategy.

Since there is never an ante in satellites, the only difference in playing no-limit and pot-limit satellites is that in pot-limit, you can only bet the size of the pot. You can play the same strategy in both types of games. By the time you really begin playing in the later stages of a pot-limit satellite, the blinds are so high and there are so many chips at stake that it is almost like playing no-limit.

REBUY TOURNAMENTS

A good way to practice for playing bigger buy-in freezeout tournaments is playing low-limit rebuy events. You can rebuy during the first three hours in most small buy-in rebuy tournaments, which can give you experience playing for a longer period of time than you might be able to play in a freezeout event.

Suppose you're playing in a $500 tournament, and you can only rebuy for $500. When the blinds get up to $25/$50, it really isn't feasible to rebuy for $500 since the blinds can eat you alive. I think that the rebuy setup that Amarillo Slim once used is better. In his rebuy tournament, the first rebuy was for $200; the second rebuy was $500; and all of the subsequent rebuys were $1,000. This was a good structure because the rebuy always gave you enough money to play at the higher limits.

You should get a pretty big percentage of return on your investment in a tournament—that's what tournaments are all about. You want to get a good overlay on your money. If the amount that you can win at the end of the tournament isn't at least fifty times the amount of money that you have put in, it really isn't a good tournament for you. So, if you pay $1,000 to enter a tournament, you want to be able to win $50,000.

I especially like the rebuy and add-on options for no-limit tournaments because no-limit is the only type of game where you can get broke on one hand. It can happen in pot-limit, but it usually doesn't happen at the lower levels, whereas in no-limit you can be gone at any time.

13 TIPS FOR WINNING ONLINE

Tom McEvoy

The saying goes that Omaha high-low is a low-card game, seven-card stud is a live-card game, and Texas hold'em is a high-card game. But Texas hold'em is more than simply a high-card game—it is also a positional game. That is, you must have good cards and good position in the betting sequence to be a winner at hold'em.

Keeping this highly important principle in mind, let's take a look at thirteen concepts that will lead you to the winners' circle when you're playing no-limit hold'em in your favorite online casino. T.J. and I regularly play poker online, and I am a spokesman for Pokerstars, where I play cash games and tournaments. These tips are adapted from Shane Smith's and my book, *Beat Texas Hold'em*. They are based on my years of experience playing online poker in the convenience of my home office.

1. CONCENTRATE ON STRONG STARTING HANDS & TABLE POSITION

Strong starting hands such as aces, kings, queens, and A-K can usually be played from any seating position at the table. You usually raise or reraise with these hands and try to eliminate as many players from the pot as possible. Why do you want to eliminate the competition before the flop? Because the fewer the players in the pot, the greater the chances that your big pair or A-K can win without improvement. The more players in the pot, the greater the possibility that someone will flop something, even if it is only a draw, that will beat you. With lots of players drawing at you, even if you have the best hand on the flop, you are in grave danger of getting beaten by the end of the hand.

What do we do about position? Last action is always preferred—the later you have to act in the betting sequence, the more advantage you have in each individual hand. Getting to act after everybody else gives you a chance to see what all the other players are doing before the action gets around to you. This does not mean you should play extremely weak starting hands just because you have the button. But it does mean that you can play a few more hands than you would if you had to act from an earlier position.

The earlier you have to act after the big blind, the worse your position is. Therefore you need a much stronger hand to enter the pot with when you are sitting in early position than you do in late position. The reason for this is that you may be subjected to one or more raises by the players who have the advantage of acting after you do. A hand such as 9-8 suited, which can be played in late position for one bet, is not playable from very early position because it isn't strong enough to call a raise.

When you are sitting in the small or big blind, you have the worst position of all after the flop. Always consider that you will have bad position after the flop in deciding whether your hand is strong enough to defend your blind (call a raise) in the event that someone raises before the flop. For example, suppose you have that marginal 9-8 suited mentioned above. In order to justify calling a raise from either the small or big blind, several other callers must already be in the pot. This is not a hand that you want to play heads-up against a raiser who has better position than you have.

Always keep in mind that when you are in one of the blinds, you will be in the worst betting position from the flop onward—you will not have the advantage of knowing what your opponents have on their minds after the flop. Pearl of wisdom: He who acts last acts with the best information.

2. AVOID PLAYING TOO LOOSE

One thing you will soon discover when you're playing small no-limit poker online is that most players see too many flops and play too many hands. In other words, they play loose as a goose. One possible reason is that many low-stakes players are new to the game and they want to play a lot of hands. They like action! It's a lot more fun to play than it is to fold and watch others play, right? Just remember that it isn't how many pots you play, it's how much money you win that really counts.

The way to beat these super loose, small-blind games is to play tighter than your opponents are playing. Playing tighter means that you play fewer hands than you really want to play. You also avoid playing weak or marginal hands when you are in an early position, or when the pot has been raised in front of you.

Another way to increase your win in loose low-stakes games is to avoid bluffing. In these smaller games you are going to have to show down a hand most of the time. People have a tendency to bluff too often, probably because they've watched too many televised no-limit tournaments where they've seen world-class players successfully bluff each other in critical situations. But believe me when I say that bluffing is not the way to play in small online games.

Small stakes players who are new to the game often will excuse an unsuccessful bluffing attempt by saying something like, "I didn't make my flush, so the only way I could win the pot was to bet." Wrong! The only way to lose an extra bet when you don't make your hand is to bluff-bet. You're going to get called most of the time, even if your opponent only has a low pair. In small stakes poker games, remember this cardinal rule: tight is right.

3. UNDERSTAND THE TEXTURE OF THE FLOP

The texture of the flop greatly affects whether you can continue with the hand. That is, does the flop contain two or more suited cards or connecting cards that give you or an opponent flush or straight draws? Is it a high-card flop with an ace or king? A low-card flop? A rainbow flop with no suited cards? Is this a flop that might have hit one or more of your opponents? For example, suppose Easy Ed raised before the flop and Dangerous Dan called the raise. The flop comes A-Q-4. How likely is it that either (or both) Ed or Dan has an ace or queen in their hands?

While you're reading the flop, study your opponents. If you cannot read other players, you can't beat hold'em games. Judging from their betting patterns, who has a good hand, who is on a draw, and who (if anybody) probably has the nuts or close to it? Trying to determine who has a draw, who has a pair, and who missed the flop completely is part of the fun and strategy of the game.

4. ADJUST TO THE SPEED OF THE GAME

You will soon discover that online games are much faster than casino games. In a typical walk-in casino hold'em game, about 30 to 35 hands per hour are dealt. In online games, around 50 to 55 hands per hour are dealt. The reason for this is twofold. First, the cyber dealer deals the cards must faster than a human dealer. Second, players cannot deliberate at length when it is their turn to act. Online poker rooms have a time clock with a very annoying beep that reminds players that they must act on their hands when they have delayed too long. If the player fails to act on his hand, his cards are automatically folded.

The good news is that you are able to see more hands per hour online than you can see in a casino. The other good news is that, with practice and experience, you can adjust to this faster pace. Here's a tip to remember: If you have a really tough decision to make, you have the option of requesting an additional 60 seconds, a feature that is offered on most sites. You don't have to feel so rushed that you can't make an intelligent decision. You can take an extra moment or two to think things over. Even after the time clock annoys you with its beep-beep, you can usually take at least 10 to 20 seconds more to make your decision.

Here's one other tip about playing online: Some online casinos protect a player if he gets disconnected and allow him to be declared all-in. This means that he can win the chips that are in the pot at the time of his loss of connection, assuming that he has the best hand at the showdown. Any further bets after a player has been disconnected will be placed in a side pot among the remaining players. This procedure is used in regular casinos as well as online cardrooms when a player has gone all in. However, not all Internet cardrooms allow this safety net. Some make you forfeit the hand if you get disconnected, so be sure you understand the rules of the online site. If you have an all-in protection and have been forced to use it, make sure to request a new all-in protection option. Most online casinos will provide you with one upon request.

5. TAKE NOTES WHILE YOU'RE PLAYING

Most online poker rooms offer a "notes" box that you can click on. It's a handy little device where you can store your notes in a virtual filing cabinet. Taking notes will help you determine the quality of your play, and give you a better idea of what the opposition is up to. Many times you will face different players, because players come and go with greater frequency online than they do in walk-in cardrooms. However, you often will find the same people playing at certain games and limits, and frequently at the same time of day. These are the types of players for whom you need your note-taking ability the most. Just typing a few quick thoughts, such as "Joe Blow just played Q-4 suited in first position," can help you get a better idea about how your opponents play and the types of hands they enter the pot with. The more you know about your opponents, the better your chances of beating them.

6. LOOK FOR TELLS

I realize that you can't see your opponents when playing online but that doesn't mean there are no tells to be discovered online. Let's take a look at a few of them. Most sites have little spaces on the screen that say, "Fold to any bet," "Raise any bet," "Automatic check," or even "Check and fold." For example, suppose you have seen the flop in a hold'em hand. You have flopped a pair, but are uncertain whether you have the best pair, so you decide to check. If all the players who act after you rapidly check, that's a sign that they have hit the automatic check button, which is usually a sign of weakness. This means that your pair is probably the best hand, at least for the moment, and you can consider betting it on the next round.

Other online players take a long time to act on their hands, and then come out betting or raising. If you pay attention to the hands they show down when they do this, you can figure out whether they usually have a big hand when they've hesitated before acting. If it always indicates a strong hand at the showdown, play accordingly. If it doesn't always mean strength, then don't put too much importance on it. People who are playing online often are also doing something else at the same time, such as reading or answering e-mail, chatting with the other players, running to the bathroom, watching television, or any number of other things that could cause the delay. Pay close attention so that you can make an informed decision as to whether the delays have any serious meaning.

7. PLAY SMALL TOURNAMENTS AT FIRST

If you're a tournament junkie like me, I suggest that you begin your online tournament career by playing one of the numerous online tournaments that are available around the clock. As a general rule, begin by playing small buy-in tournaments. Why? To create a comfort zone for yourself as a fledgling tournament player. If you do well in the smaller buy-in events against weaker opponents, your confidence will steadily increase, and then you can think about stepping up. If you are successful in tournaments and learn to love them as I do, then you can increase the parameters of your comfort zone and play bigger buy-in events.

You will find tournaments you can enter for as little as $1 and as high as $530 on a regular basis, with all sorts of buy-ins in between those numbers. Some sites even offer freerolls in which all the money is put up by the site for its customers. I have seen as many as 30,000 players playing in the same freeroll tournament online.

Whew!

Just try conquering that size field some time! Poker has a way of teaching all of us humility.

Playing small buy-in, one-table tournaments—sit'n'gos or one-table satellites—online can be great learning experiences. For a limited investment, you can get a good idea about what kinds of hands people play and how they perform in different situations. Since you can't pull more money out of your pocket to buy more chips, you limit your expenses and prevent yourself from spending more money than you planned on by playing these small events.

Another advantage of playing one-table tournaments and satellites is that they give you experience playing short-handed, so you will have a much better feel for what to do when you make it to the final table of a multi-table tournament.

8. SCHEDULE YOUR TOURNAMENT PLAY

Because there are so many tournaments to choose from, you need to choose the ones that suit your bankroll and your time requirements. Don't sign up for a tournament that will take four hours to complete if you have to be somewhere else in two hours. Why bother to play in the first place if you don't have the time to finish? If it's worth playing at all, the tournament requires your best effort and enough free time to finish the job if you are lucky enough to go the distance.

I like to pencil in on my calendar the tournaments on the various sites that I am especially interested in. This way I can try to arrange my schedule to be available for as many of them as possible. I note the site, the game, the buy-in, the date, the starting time, and anything else that might be of interest. Many online poker rooms offer special promotions and tournament deals that are too good to pass up. By checking a site's upcoming events, I can choose the best bargains and put them on my schedule.

9. DON'T PLAY TO ESCAPE FROM SOMETHING

When you have a lot of other things on your mind, it is very difficult to focus on poker. If you've had an argument with somebody significant, it's hard to get it off your agenda so that you can concentrate and play your best game. If you insist on playing anyway, like so many of us do, then at least play in a smaller game where you won't hurt your bankroll too much if you lose.

Above all, don't kid yourself into thinking that you can play a good game of poker when you're distracted or bothered by something. Even the best of players can't play their "A" game when they're stressed. Fortunately for the top players, their "B" game or (true story) even their "C" game is often better than most of the players they are competing against. But most of us are best advised to pass under stress It's tough enough to win when you are focused and paying attention, so don't handicap yourself even more by playing when something is weighing heavily on your mind.

10. DON'T PLAY WITH MORE MONEY THAN YOU CAN AFFORD TO LOSE

This tip is ignored or forgotten more often than any of the other tips. Why? I think it's because, in the heat of battle, we often chase after our losses. Sometimes we play higher than we should, other times we start playing bad poker. We go on tilt like the old-fashioned pinball machines used to do when they malfunctioned. We start making bad choices in starting hands, chasing with the worst cards, calling or even raising when we should fold you get the message. Play within your financial comfort zone. Don't play in games that have bigger stakes than you can afford, or bigger stakes than you feel comfortable at playing.

I know a multimillionaire who can afford to play in the biggest games in Las Vegas, yet he isn't comfortable playing any higher than $20/$40 limit games. Then there's Bill Gates, the founder of MicroSoft. Gates has been known to step into a casino poker room from time to time where he usually plays $3/$6 poker. That's $3/$6, not buildings or oil wells like he could afford to play if he chose.

Remember that once you have booked some wins, the money in your online account is real money—it spends just like money you earned at your job, and it is yours to keep or to reinvest. Do not give it back, and do not put more money in your online account that you can afford to lose.

One way you can avoid giving it back is quitting the game when you know you should. No matter how good the game, it's not a good game for you if you're losing. I use a very simple formula that governs when to quit the game. It is this—never lose more in one session than you can reasonably expect to win in your next session. The formula assumes, of course, that you are playing the same form of poker at the same limits. For example a good win in a $5/$10 limit game is around $200. If you are losing more than $200, which is 20 big bets, it's time to call it a day. Around 20 big bets is about the most you should ever lose in one session. You don't have to limit your wins, however; play as long the game is still good and you're not too tired. The idea is to not limit your wins, but definitely limit your losses.

If you find yourself going on tilt because you've taken a few bad beats, it's time to leave. Another reason to quit is because some of the weaker players have left the game and have been replaced by much tougher opponents. If you think you are no longer a favorite to win in the game, for any reason whatsoever, it's time to fold up your tent and hit the "I quit" button.

11. THE PLAY CHANGES IN HIGHER LIMIT ONLINE GAMES

Online no-limit hold'em games with bigger blinds, such as $3/$6 and higher, play much differently than lower stakes games. Better players, including some professionals, are usually in these games, and the bigger blinds mean more to shoot for in each pot. Far fewer players call raises to see a flop in these games compared to the smaller games, so there are fewer hands to beat, though your opponents usually play better quality starting hands.

Bluffing becomes more of a factor in the bigger games. With more money in the pot to begin with and fewer players seeing the flop, only two or three players usually are contesting each pot. Since everyone who has not started with a high pair needs to improve, it's good to remember that each person fails to help his hand about 70 percent of the time on the flop. Therefore, continuation bets are far more common.

A continuation bet is a bet that you make against only one or two opponents no matter what the flop is and regardless of whether it helped your hand or not. You're basically counting on your opponents missing the flop and being willing to fold to your bet. I would caution against overdoing this play, as sooner or later your opponents will catch on and start raising you with weak hands to resteal the pot.

12. TAKE ADVANTAGE OF YOUR TABLE IMAGE

Always be aware of your table image. If you are perceived as a tight player, bluff more. If you have been caught bluffing once or twice, don't bluff anymore, just wait for a strong hand and milk it for all it is worth. Think about your opponents' table images. Try to get inside their heads and put yourself in their place. What do they think of you? What do they think you think of them? Ego has destroyed more bankrolls than anything else. You are there to get the money, not show off. Online players are notorious for being oblivious of the true goals of playing poker.

Mike Caro has described a behavior known as FPS. That stands for fancy play syndrome and falls in the category of showing off to your opponents. You want them to think you're a very clever player and can outplay them. This does not work against opponents who are unaware of what you are doing. And of course, professional players usually catch on quickly to what you're up to, so be very careful when you make a tricky play. Make your fancy plays against players that you think it will work against, not someone who isn't paying attention.

13. REMAIN FOCUSED AND IN THE MOMENT

No-limit hold'em is a very unforgiving game. Make one mistake at a crucial time and you're out of the tournament. It is of the utmost importance that you pay attention when playing online events. You can't go eyeball to eyeball with your opponents, so you need to take notes and be aware when a new player sits down at the table. Players who come in with a lot of chips either got very lucky or played extremely well at another table to accumulate them. Try to figure out as soon as possible which it is. Sometimes it is a little of both.

Online tournaments have both advantages and disadvantages when compared to walk-in casinos. The advantages are that you can play in the comfort of your home, take proper notes unnoticed, and take short breaks when you want. You also get to see more hands per hour. The disadvantages are that you can't actually see your opponents, which makes it tougher to accurately evaluate them. You have shorter playing time before the blinds and antes increase, and you also have less time to act on your hand, so everything moves at a much faster pace. For players who need a little more time to think things through, this is a definite disadvantage.

But whether you're playing online or in a walk-in casino, your best bet is to stay focused and in the moment, especially in tournament play.

HOW TO WIN AT POT-LIMIT HOLD'EM

These chapters on pot-limit hold'em are designed especially for you players who are looking for some diversity in your game selection. Pot-limit hold'em is one of my favorite games—try it and you'll like it, guaranteed!

In pot-limit hold'em, you can bet what is in the pot at any time, but only what is in the pot at that time. In straight pot-limit, if there is a $5 and a $10 blind, the first player in the pot can call the $10 and raise $25. The second player can call the size of the pot, or raise the size of the pot with his bet in it. For example, if there's $35 in the pot, he can call the $35, and then raise $70 for a total bet of $105, making the total in the pot $140. If a player wishes to reraise, he can call the $140 and raise $280. This is how the pot grows fast.

HOW POT-LIMIT DIFFERS FROM NO-LIMIT

Pot-limit hold'em is a great game when it is played with a high blind structure. No-limit is a great game with any blind structure. The main difference between the two games is that in pot-limit, because of the size of the bets that you are forced to make, you cannot run people out of the pot with a big bet like you can do in no-limit. In no-limit, you can protect your hand (if you want to) by putting in a big raise. No-limit hold'em is an aggressive game. Pot-limit is a semi-aggressive game.

You usually cannot protect big pairs before the flop in pot-limit. An exception occurs when you limp in, somebody raises, and another player reraises. In this case, you can raise again so as to get some people out of the pot.

You have more opportunities to make trap plays in pot-limit than in no-limit. And in pot-limit, you can raise with some hands that you can't raise with in no-limit. But after that, your aggression should shut down a little bit. There are a lot of players taking shots with the same hands in pot-limit and you can get yourself in a trap, whereas in no-limit, you can bet enough money to put people to a test every time.

THE PROTECTION FEATURE

One of the main features of pot-limit hold'em is its protection procedure. It is a game designed for people who will take flops to hands like 4-5, 5-6, or 7-8 suited for a minimum amount of money. If a player brings it in for $40 and you can play for just $40, you might be able to take someone off who has a big hand. If an opponent has two aces or two kings, for example, and the flop comes out 3-6-7, he usually won't give you credit for 4-5, and he'll come out betting. A lot of times, then, you can trap an opponent in pot-limit, whereas you can't trap as much in no-limit because it costs you too much to make that call. Because of this, a lot of people prefer pot-limit to no-limit hold'em.

Pot-limit is a game that gives you a chance to play a lot of little pairs. It is designed for that. Some aggressive players often put in small raises, hoping to flop to their hands. For a minimum bet, the size of the big blind in an unraised pot, or four times the big blind if someone brings it in for that amount, you can play pocket sixes or sevens—and you might flop a set. Pot-limit is completely different from no-limit in this respect.

GOALS IN POT-LIMIT HOLD'EM

Your main goal in pot-limit hold'em is maximizing the amount of money that you can win on a hand. A good pot-limit player can maximize his win with correct betting sequences. If you have a hand that you can raise with, do it. You want to build the pot, *not* limit the field.

When you have the chips and you have the hand that you want to play, you won't be giving away any information if you always bet the size of the pot. If you always bet the size of the pot, your opponents can't get a tell on what kind of hand you have. A big-time player that I know has the biggest tell in the world: When he makes a baby raise, he has a big hand, and when he makes a big raise, he has a marginal hand. This reverse tell of his is as pure as driven snow. He's always afraid that he won't get called if he puts in a big raise when he has a big hand.

In addition to the small pairs, some players will even try to sweeten the pot with a little pot-builder raise with hands like J-10 or 9-8 suited. They're hoping to build a pot with their modest raises to make sure that there's a little something in the pot in case they hit a hand. There's nothing wrong with this strategy *if* you're a good enough player to get away from a hand.

Say that you raise with J-10 and get two or three callers. Then the flop comes J-4-5.

YOU

FLOP

How do you play the hand? That's the big question. If you bet and get any action on the hand, there's a pretty good chance that you're beaten already. So, you have to be skilled enough to know when your hand is good and when it isn't. And that goes back to your observation skills, and knowing how other people play.

Many times you will just check this hand because you want to find out where you are. Any time that you hear somebody say, "I made a bet to find out where I was," you know that person is making a bad play. Listen carefully: It is foolish to put money into a pot to find out where you are. You should be observant enough and play well enough to find that out without having to put up any money.

How often have you heard a player say that he bet $200 at a pot because he "wanted to see where I was." To me, that is a ridiculous statement in poker. Why would you ever do something like that? Suppose you put in $200 and some guy raises you. What are you going to do with the hand? You're going to throw it away. But if you had checked and the man then made a decent bet, you would know that he had some kind of hand. Then it's up to you whether you want to call him. You sure wouldn't have wasted that $200!

DOES THE SIZE OF THE BLINDS AFFECT STRATEGY?

Does the size of the game affect the way that you play? My theory is that it does not. Say that you have your choice of three pot-limit games: a $5/$10, a $10/$10, and a $10/$25. To play the $10/$25 game, of course you should have a big enough bankroll to feel comfortable. Even if your bankroll is four or five times the amount you need to play the game, you're still going to play it the same way. You should play the same hands, no matter what the structure. In side games, your strategy should not be affected by the size of the blinds.

Personally, I like to play in games with a high blind structure because then I can get more protection for my hands. You should have the same standards for the hands that you play regardless of the size of game you're playing. Some people will play looser when they're playing in cheaper games and play hands that aren't as good as they would play in higher limit games, because they figure that it isn't costing them much to play. They are the losers. If your standards are the same for every size of game you play, you're going to get the money.

A good player doesn't hope to get a 60/40 break in the cards. If the cards break even, a good player will win the money—at all times—because he's going to make fewer mistakes than a bad player will make. What does poker break down to in the long run? Most of the money you make comes from somebody's mistakes. Good players also make mistakes, but they make fewer of them.

In tournament play, though, the size of the blinds does affect your play. As you progress in a tournament, you will have more chips—or you won't progress. As the blinds increase, your chips should increase. Of course, the rise in blinds shouldn't affect your play a lot, but you do have to be a little bit more selective on your starting hands. Hold'em is a position game, and you're going to play your position strong as the levels go up, no matter what the blinds are.

WHO PLAYS POT-LIMIT HOLD'EM?

Four different categories of players enter pot-limit hold'em tournaments. There are players like Freddy Deeb and the late Stu Ungar who are super aggressive; they are going to play more hands than the whole table combined will play. They stand raises with hands that a lot of players would fold. They either amass a lot of chips or they're out of the tournament early. Then there are the semi-aggressive players. I classify myself in this category. I'm semi-aggressive in the middle stages of the tournament, but I am very aggressive late in the tournament.

There are also passive players and defensive players. The passive player will play pots but he never leads at the pot. Usually, he's playing from behind, letting somebody else bet for him. If he has a K-10 in his hand and the board comes K-10-8, he doesn't lead with the hand, and he doesn't raise on the flop if somebody else bets. He's afraid that a queen or a jack will come off on the turn and make a straight for an opponent. Consequently, he doesn't get full value from his hands. He may last a long time in the tournament, but he never gets enough chips to win the event.

The defensive player is usually a scared player. He becomes intimidated by playing at a table with known players. You know he's afraid even before the cards are dealt. I hear it a lot: "Oh no, don't tell me I have to play at the table with so-and-so." Defensive players don't usually make it to the final table. If you're a strong player, you have them at a disadvantage even before the tournament begins. You know that in the right spot, you can make them lay down a hand.

STARTING HANDS: WHAT AND WHY

To play from an early position in pot-limit hold'em, you should have an A-Q suited or better. From a middle position, fifth spot and later, you might play A-J or A-10 suited and up. From a late position into the blinds, you can play K-10 suited and above.

We all know that big pairs are the strongest starting hands in hold'em. But when some players rate starting hands, they rank them in this order: A-A, K-K, A-K, Q-Q. They put A-K before Q-Q. I don't!

I rate the big-card starting hands as A-A, K-K, Q-Q, J-J, 10-10 and *then* A-K. I realize that some computer people rank A-K higher, but if you play day-to-day, you'll see the value in ranking Big Slick below the high pairs.

The reason that I go all the way down to tens before throwing in Big Slick is because you can still make the nut straight with a 10. Plus, you will make more nut straights (ace high) with a 10 than with any other card. With tens, you can make the A-K-Q-J-10 straight, all the way down to the 10-9-8-7-6 straight—and those hands do come up. That is why I rate a pair of tens above A-K as a starting hand.

These are opening hands. They are not necessarily hands that you would call with. Of course, you will play these hands plus some others when three or four players are already in the pot. Keep in mind that in unraised pots, it takes pretty much the same standards to call a pot as it does to open it.

Playing Small Pairs

You also can start with small pairs, depending on the size of the pair, your position, and the action. You might play hands like deuces, treys, fours, or fives, from fifth position or later. Suppose you're in fifth or sixth position in a $10/$10 game, a player has brought it in for a small raise of $40, and three players are in the pot. The pot is laying you good odds, so why not call the $40 with your small pocket pair? If you flop a set, you're probably going to win a good-sized pot. If you don't flop a set, you can get away from it and all it has cost you is your original bet.

It is the weak players who trap themselves with the small pairs. Say that the flop comes J-8-6 and a player bets on the flop. The weak player is holding a pair of fours and he calls, hoping to catch a four on the turn. That is a horrible play. For the number of times that you will catch your card in that instance, you might lose thirty times. And even if you do catch it, you might be up against a larger set and end up losing your whole bankroll. Calling with an underpair on the flop is limit strategy, and limit strategy doesn't work in pot-limit hold'em.

When you're in a rammin'-jammin' game where there's a lot of preflop raising, the small pairs and suited connectors don't play very well because it gets to be too expensive to see the flop with them. But when you're in a normal pot-limit game where there's a lot of limping going on and just an average amount of raising, you can limp in with the small pairs out of position, even from an early position.

Tom and I differ on how we play small pairs. He will call a small raise if it looks like he's going to get multiway action on his small pair. For example, if a couple of people have limped and then a player raises the pot to $40 or $50, the gamble is worth it because the implied odds are there. Sometimes, your call of a small raise will attract other callers and then you are almost guaranteed to get a good price on your hand. So what if you miss the flop? You're only in there for a small amount and you have the chance to win a big pot.

I have a different line of thinking. I believe that when you compare the number of times that you will flop a hand with your small pair and get a play on the hand after the flop, with the number of times that you will burn up $40 or $50 making the call, the numbers don't even out. In the long run, I think that you will be a loser to the small pairs. If you catch a set to the small pair, you have to get a play on the flop. You might go twenty or thirty hands without hitting a flop. Unless you have a big cash reserve in a pot-limit ring game, you can run through a lot of money that way.

Playing Small Suited Connectors

Pot-limit is designed for playing suited connectors for the same reason that it is designed for playing small pairs—when you can get in cheaply. Say that you are on the button with 4-5 suited, the pot has been raised, three or four people have called the pot, and it costs you $40 to call. You can take a flop to this type of hand for $40. You might flop the nuts and break somebody who is holding a big overpair. If you don't flop to it, it's the easiest hand in the world to get away from.

Taking flops with small connectors can be especially profitable in side games. You might flop two pair, three-of-a-kind, or a straight with them, all of which can be good hands. If you watch a great player like Bobby Hoff playing in side games, you'll notice that when he's on the button with two connectors, he usually brings it in for a baby raise. The cards don't even need to be suited.

Computer runs say that suited connectors are always better than unsuited connectors. But the computer doesn't factor into the equation that there may be three or four other players in the pot who could be holding cards in your same suit—and there's a good chance of that happening. My thinking in pot-limit is that when you play connectors, they don't necessarily need to be suited because when they are suited, they can become trap hands. There is more value in the cards being *connected* than in being suited. In fact, a lot of times, you don't want to be suited with those small connectors because if the flop comes two to a suit, there's a chance that you might be up against a higher flush draw, and then the hand can cost you a lot of money.

We don't favor suited connectors as much in the early positions because you usually have to make a lot of tricky judgment plays. Sometimes, you'll make something with your hand and still have to muck it, especially when you flop a flush draw. Other times, you'll flop top pair with a straight draw, but you're out of position—and then what do you do?

The broke player's lament as he's walking out the door from a pot-limit or no-limit game is "I lost a big pot calling with such-and-such hand. But I was suited." Big deal! There are a lot of times when your suit comes up, but many times, it doesn't. Of course, if you have A-K suited against A-K offsuit, you're a favorite. You're a *slight* favorite, but still you are a favorite for the few times that the flop comes in your suit.

When you're heads-up in a raised pot, you cannot call with the connectors. The pot has to be laying you odds to play them—that means three or four players in the pot. You don't want to be heads-up with a drawing hand where you have to get lucky to flop to it. When you're heads-up, you want to have a hammer. That's why I don't play the connectors in tournaments. I always try to play top hands rather than drawing hands.

Playing Two Big Cards

When can you play two big cards in pot-limit hold'em? I prefer having the action passed to me when I'm in one of the back four positions. When you call with two big cards from a late position, there is a fairly good chance that you won't get raised. Even if you do, you have only called the original bet and you can get away from the hand easily. When I'm in late position, I might play marginal hands that I normally wouldn't play–K-Q, K-J, or K-10, for example—with the idea of folding against a preflop raise, or folding on the flop if I need to.

The problem that many players cause for themselves is playing any two big cards from any position. That is not a good idea. Let's start with A-J, one of the biggest trash hands you can play. To illustrate why I don't think very highly of A-J, take a look at this situation. Say that you've come into the pot for a little raise with an A-J offsuit. Or maybe you're playing in an unraised pot with three or four players in it. The flop comes A-8-4 rainbow.

YOU

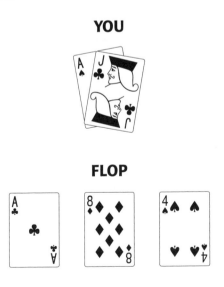

FLOP

Looks pretty good, huh? Not at all. You can get trapped very easily with A-J. You might be against A-K, A-Q, two pair (A-4 is the most likely), or any set. From an early position in side games, you're way better off dumping A-J. And hands such as K-J, K-Q, and K-10 also are dangerous. If you don't flop a straight to them, or flop a full house to them (when you flop two of one rank and one of the other rank), you're in trouble.

What do you want to catch to these kinds of hands? You don't want to make top pair because chances are that you'll be outkicked, or somebody might hold an overpair. I prefer playing the small and medium connectors over two big cards. Of course, if it's passed to you on the button when the only hands to act after you are the blinds, then these hands might have some value. But in early positions, they are bad hands.

Suppose you flat call before the flop with K-J, and only the two blinds and you are in the pot on the flop. The flop comes K-4-2.

YOU

FLOP

If one of the two blinds leads at the pot, you probably would just flat call; but if they both check, then you would bet. The reason you just flat call the blind's bet in an unraised pot is because he could have any two random cards and might have flopped two pair (K-4, K-2, or 4-2). Changing the situation, suppose the flop comes K-10-2 in an unraised pot.

YOU

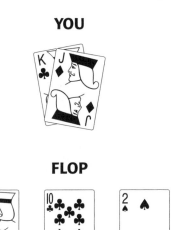

FLOP

It wouldn't be unusual for the blind to lead at the pot with second pair, especially if he is holding cards such as A-10 offsuit. The small or big blind is the place from which a lot of players will bet second pair in an unraised pot. With your K-J, you can be fairly sure that you have the best hand, as well as the chance to knock your opponent off. I don't suggest that you raise with the hand; just call. Then if your opponent shuts down on fourth street, you can bet. Or you can play to win just the one bet on the flop. In an unraised pot, there is nothing wrong with just playing to win a small pot on the flop so that you don't get yourself trapped.

What About Ace-Small Suited?

Is there a time when you would play ace-small suited in pot-limit hold'em? Sure there is—when you can get in cheaply in an unraised pot. That's one of the main ideas in pot-limit hold'em. If you can get in for a cheap price, why not take a flop to ace-small suited? You can come into an unraised pot from any position with the hand, and then if someone raises behind you, you can throw it away without losing many chips.

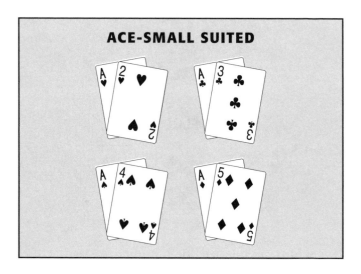

Remember that when you are playing ace-small (A-2, A-3, A-4, A-5), you can make a number of hands, including the nut flush, a straight, or two pair. Sometimes you can even make a small set such as three deuces, treys, fours, or fives. The nice thing is that all of these sets have the top kicker, the ace, to go with them.

Can You Play High Three-Gap Hands?

One of the differences between playing pot-limit and no-limit hold'em tournaments is that players will try to steal pots with high three-gappers in no-limit events once they reach the $100/$200 blinds with an ante level. But in pot-limit tournaments, there is never an ante. Therefore, picking up pots in pot-limit hold'em tournaments does not have the value it has in no-limit events because, without the antes, there isn't as much to pick up.

So, playing hands such as K-9 is a no-no. In fact, you don't play any three-gap hands in pot-limit hold'em. Sure, you can flop a straight to hands like K-9 or Q-8 suited, 9-5 or 7-3, but you can never make the *nut* straight. Although a lot of people play them, I don't play three-gappers, period.

Just for your information: In poker, the K-9 is called "sawmill." Here's a true story about how it got that name. Cowboy Wolford and Milton Butts were playing up in the hill country in Texas and Cowboy had gotten broke in the game. So, they were driving down a hill going out of town when they passed by a big lumber camp. Cowboy looked over at Milton and said, "Even those guys working in that sawmill wouldn't have got broke on a K-9."

And that hand has been called a "sawmill" ever since then.

THE PURPOSE OF THE PREFLOP ACTION

With a good hand, the purpose of the preflop action in pot-limit hold'em is to build a pot. The preflop action in no-limit hold'em is much bigger because you can get all of your chips in the pot before the flop, but that usually isn't the case in pot-limit.

You might have the same criteria for starting hands in no-limit that you have in pot-limit, but you have to be much more careful with them in no-limit because any time you play a hand, your entire pile of chips is at risk. In pot-limit, it is not. In no-limit side games, a lot more hands are won without seeing a flop than happens in pot-limit side games. That is because you can't put as much pressure on your opponents before the flop. Therefore, you'll see a lot more flops in pot-limit hold'em.

Since a lot more people see flops, there are more multiway pots in pot-limit cash games, especially when several players have deep pockets and are liberal with their preflop action. This is what makes the pot-limit side games during a tournament so juicy. If you make the nuts against liberal players, you'll get action from them, whereas in no-limit, you're usually up against just one guy and you won't get the action that you want. The multiway pot feature of pot-limit hold'em is another reason why you can play the suited connectors and the small pairs more often. For some players, playing those little cards is the thrill of the game.

WHICH HANDS CAN YOU RAISE WITH?

Although you can raise the pot for any amount up to the size of the pot, I suggest that you always raise the amount of the pot. The only thing that would stop me from raising the size of the pot is if I didn't have enough money in front of me. In that case, I would raise all-in.

The raising hands in pot-limit are the standard raising hands in all of hold'em: A-A, K-K, on down to A-K. But because pot-limit hold'em is a structured game, I probably will bring in the hand for a minimum raise ($40 in a $10/$10 blinds game) with 9-9 or above. If someone reraises, whether I call depends upon my observation of the players. Who does what in which situations?

For example, 9-9 isn't much of a hand to call a reraise with, but it's an easy hand to get away from if you don't flop to it. A lot of times, a liberal player will stand a reraise with a pair of nines. If he has brought it in for $40, the reraiser can call the $40 raise and reraise it $100. The three blinds are in for $5, $5, and $10 and you have raised it by $40, making $60 in the pot. Adding the $40 required to call your raise, the reraiser can raise the pot by $100. So, the original raiser often will call the reraise and take a flop with pocket nines because it only costs him $100 more to try to flop a set and win the pot.

Now suppose Player A has brought it in for a raise and you have called the raise with K-K. Then Player C reraises behind you. What do you do? You have all kinds of options. You might just flat call Player A's raise, but when Player C reraises behind you, you have to decide whether you have the best hand. A lot of times, against average players, your kings will be the best hand and you're going to call Player C's reraise. But you should not take the option of reraising the pot again, because you might be up against two aces.

You also want to see if an ace hits the flop before you commit a lot more money to this pot, so you just flat call before the flop with your kings. If an ace doesn't hit the flop, and if you don't put an opponent on aces, you probably have the best hand—unless somebody flops a set, in which case the action will tell you what to do next.

WHEN NOT TO CALL A RAISE

There are situations when you won't call a raise before the flop. Suppose that Player C raises on the button and one of the blinds pops it again. Unless you have a pair of aces, you probably shouldn't call; you should throw away your kings.

You don't have much invested in the pot and even if he doesn't have aces, it's not a bad play to fold the kings. Where I was schooled in Dallas, the second raise probably would have been aces, and the third raise was like Ivory snow: 99.9 percent pure aces. It's not A-K in this situation: It's A-A.

Whether you call or fold gets back to knowing your opponents. You know that some of them are loose enough to put in the third raise with two queens, so now your only question is, "Was he lucky enough to pick up two aces in this pot, or do I have the best hand?" Then you make your decision. There are other players you know who would never put in the third raise without two aces. In that case, it's easy to dump the kings. In fact, I dumped them in two different hands against a single raise during the World Series of Poker in 1985. I raised the pot, Mike Allen reraised, and I threw them away both times—and both times, Allen showed me two aces.

A top player that I know likes to reraise with Q-Q because he says the raise helps him find out where he is in the hand. If his opponent comes over the top of him, he knows his hand is no good. I don't like his reasoning. You're supposed to know where you're at without have to put money in the pot. Even if you're in a game with a lot of players that you don't know, you should be able to get a line on each of them within the first fifteen minutes of the game.

Which brings me to probe bets. I think probe bets are some of the worst plays in all of hold'em. Why would you want to sacrifice money to find out where you are in a hand? And that's the definition of a probe bet—you're probing to see where are in a hand. By their actions and their betting patterns, your opponents will inform you or let you know where they are in the hand. You don't have to lose any money—betting second pair, for example—to find out information. My thinking is that if you bet second pair to see where you are, you're out of it.

But if you bet second pair to try to win the pot, that's a whole different ballgame.

THE CHECK-RAISE

Good players always try to maximize their bets in pot-limit to win all that they can get out of a hand. If you're playing check-raise, you're always taking the chance that your opponent won't bet. Then, if you have a big hand, what will you win in that pot?

For that reason, the check-raise is used far less often in pot-limit hold'em than it is in no-limit hold'em.

CALLING A RAISE FROM THE BLINDS

A *player* does not stand raises with a weak hand in the blinds; a non-player does. The non-player says to himself, "It's only costing me $30 more (depending on the limits). Since it's only a minimum raise and I have J-10, I'll just call and take off a card." That kind of thinking burns up a lot of money.

You would need to hit the perfect flop to win with a hand such as J-10. Making top pair (jacks) is no good because you have no kicker. One of the only two times that you can play the hand is when you know that your opponent makes a token raise with any small pair; then you might look at the flop. If it comes with a jack, you might bet because you know that your opponent is overly aggressive and may have raised with a baby pair such as 3-3.

The other time you can play this hand from the blind is when your opponent is the type of player who always bets on the button when it is checked to him. In this case, you might come back over the top of him from the blind with J-10 and win the pot right there. Of course, every time you do that, you need to be right. And the man on the button has to be a decent player, one that you know will lay down a hand against a raise.

Moving right along in the action, let's take a look at some flops in pot-limit hold'em and analyze how best to play them.

HOW TO BUILD THE POT ON THE FLOP IN POT-LIMIT

BASIC PRINCIPLES

The art of pot-limit hold'em lies in knowing how to build the pot. That's the whole idea of the game. Your goal is to maximize the amount of money that you can make when you have a winning hand. That's why slow-playing on the flop doesn't make much sense.

Say that you flop a big hand and you check on the flop. All of your opponents also check. The net result is that on fourth street, you can only bet the amount that you could have bet on the flop. Now let's say that you bet on the flop and get a call or two to build the pot. With that added money in the pot, your next bet can be a pretty good-sized wager. You're maximizing what you can win as you go along with the hand.

You can slow-play hands a lot more often in no-limit because you can bet any amount that you want at any time. But in pot-limit, with its structured bets, you have to *build* the amount that you can bet. You're not looking to set a trap with the slow play—you want people to play with you. So, you lead with your sets and hope that somebody will play back at you.

If they don't play back, you're hoping that they will at least call because your next bet is going to be larger and you want them to call again.

If your opponents are still with you as you progress through the betting stages, you can always bet more as you go along. And that is how you maximize the amount that you can win on the hand.

Suppose you come into a hand with J-J. The flop comes K-J-4.

YOU

FLOP

Let's say that you check on the flop. But why? Are you hoping that someone will bet it for you so that you can put in a raise and shut out your opponent? Wrong!

If you lead with the hand, nobody will know for sure what you have. If someone flat calls you, that's okay because he doesn't know for sure where you're at. And you're getting more money into the pot so that you can lead at it again. Or somebody might raise you, in which case your best play (with the king on the board) may be to just call—not because you're afraid that he has trip kings, but because you don't want to blow him out of the pot. You still want to build that pot!

If you are raised on the flop and you just flat call, there is a decent amount of money in the pot on fourth street. Now you might want to check, let him make the bet, and then go over the top of him with a raise—you have him pot-committed.

Of course, there are a lot of ways to play any hand, but when you have a big hand, always keep in mind that your goal is to maximize what you can win in the pot. You don't want to take the chance of flopping a big hand and just winning $40 with it. That happens a lot of times, and sometimes you can't help it—that is, when you lead and they throw their hands away, so that all you win is what is in the pot.

Another reason that you want to lead at the pot with your jacks against the K-J-4 flop is that you don't want to give your opponents a cheap draw at you. With a couple of suited connectors on the board, someone could easily have a wraparound straight draw or a flush draw. You want to force them put some money in the pot to make their draws. Make them pay to play! Then if the possible straight or flush comes, you can always get away from your hand.

In pot-limit, you can't shut your opponents out of the pot with a huge bet like you can in no-limit hold'em. But you can make it expensive enough that they won't be able to draw at you cheaply. A big part of your strategy in pot-limit is to manipulate the size of the pot with your bets.

Build the pot and take it down!

PLAYING SECOND PAIR ON THE FLOP

Suppose that a couple of players have checked on the flop, you have second pair, and it's up to you. I don't suggest that you bet it right there. You can take off another card and get a little more information on the hand without putting any money into the pot. Believe me, another card will give you a lot more information, and you won't be taking any chances in case you're playing against guys who like to check-raise.

If you know that your opponents are likely to check-raise and lay traps, you are less likely to bet than if they are playing straightforward poker, in which case you have more reason to bet. It all goes back to knowing your opponents.

GETTING BROKE IN AN UNRAISED POT? IT CAN HAPPEN!

One of your biggest worries in pot-limit hold'em is getting broke in an unraised pot. This happens more often than not when you flop top pair against an opponent who limped into the pot with an inferior hand. Of course, if you flop top pair with top kicker in an unraised pot, you will be putting in a bet.

For example, let's say that you have A-9 suited or offsuit, you're in one of the blinds, and you got in cheaply. The flop comes 9-2-5 rainbow.

YOU

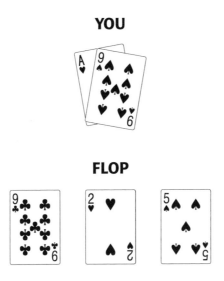

FLOP

You have top pair, top kicker. Even from a front position, you have to bet your hand. Why? Because in an unraised pot, there is better than a 75 percent chance that you have the best hand. The only thing you have to worry about is that someone has limped into the pot with two deuces or fives and flops a set or two pair—probably from one of the blinds—since you're playing in an unraised pot.

A player also could have a 3-4 suited, but you would like that. First of all, you have the ace in your hand, which is one of his straight cards. Secondly, any time that you are a 2 to 1 favorite in a hand, you want your opponents to draw. If they make it, they make it, but you have the best of it. So, with this type of flop, you definitely want to lead out with your A-9.

I am discussing the A-9, specifically, because you are likely to limp in with it in an unraised pot if a lot of players have limped in front of you. Now suppose the flop comes 9-5-2, you bet, and an opponent calls. A king comes on the turn.

YOU

TURN

Should that scare you? No, not in pot-limit or no-limit hold'em. If you get called on the flop, it probably means that somebody has something with the 9; that is, they have a draw, or maybe even a pair in a rank between fives and nines (a pair of sevens, for example). Unless a player has a K-5 or K-9, why would he have called you on the flop?

In limit hold'em, that king on the turn could scare you to death, but in pot-limit and no-limit, it wouldn't. A much scarier card on the turn would be a card that's connected to the 9, a 10 or an 8.

TURN

Why is this a scary turn? Because someone could have limped in with a 9-8 suited to make two pair on the turn. Or what about a 7-6? In that case, you have no way of winning the pot. That's why a connecting card is scarier than a king.

Even a jack on the turn would be scarier than a king. Any card that connects within two holes of the 10 would be scary because most pot-limit players will play a one-holer (J-9 or Q-10, for example) or a two-holer (J-8 or Q-9), especially in tournaments. However, they will not play a three-holer such as Q-8 or J-7. And that's a good thing to remember in the next pot-limit hold'em tournament you play.

Now, suppose you have an A-Q in the blind and a lot of limpers are in the pot. With the A-Q, you probably would want to raise before the flop. When you flop top pair and a big kicker, you don't necessarily need to have the best kicker to lead out. For example, suppose the flop comes 9-5-2 and you have Q-9 in your hand.

YOU

FLOP

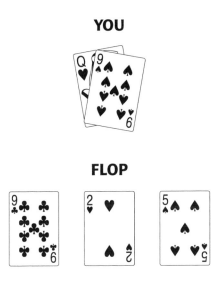

Since you got in the pot for nothing, you can lead-bet. You're not leading to find out information; you're leading to win the pot right there. You're betting it as the best hand. There's a big difference in betting your hand as the best hand and betting "to find out where you're at."

Now let's discuss some pointers on playing Big Slick, one of the most frequently misplayed hands in any form of hold'em.

WALKING BACK TO HOUSTON: PLAYING BIG SLICK

We used to say that if you play Big Slick often enough in Dallas and you live in Houston, you're gonna' have to walk the 249 miles back to Houston a few times—and for a good reason. In both pot-limit and no-limit hold'em, A-K is the type of hand that you want to win without seeing a flop. You raise with the hand, yes, but you raise *because* you want to win the money right then and there.

Suppose you're holding A-K and the flop comes K-4-6.

YOU

FLOP

You usually would lead at the pot in this situation, but there are a few occasions when you might slow-play the hand. Although I've said that you never slow-play in pot-limit hold'em, actually I should never say *never*, because even in pot-limit, there are exceptions to the rule.

For example, suppose you have raised the pot before the flop with your A-K. Some weaker players actually will call the pot with hands such as K-Q, K-J or K-10. So, why not give them one check on the flop? You know they'll come right out of their shoes if they flop top pair—and then you can get them with a check-raise. But if you are going to check-raise, you must do it on the flop so that you don't give your opponents a chance to make a second pair or something else on the turn that will beat your top pair/top kicker.

Over the years, so many players have asked, "How could you get broke with one pair?"

That is why you check-raise on the flop, without giving them a chance at making a double pair or some fantastic drawout on the turn. There are ten cards that are connected to the king, and they could be playing a queen, jack, or 10. Some bad players will even play a king with a suited 9. So when you check, they may figure, "Well, he's got something between tens and kings, so I'd better take this pot right now."

Then you've got 'em!

So much of this strategy depends upon the texture of the flop and the nature of the players at the table. Just be sure that you know your opponents well enough that you figure one of them will bet on the flop so that you can put in your check-raise.

The idea is to get your opponent pot-committed. In fact, whenever you have the top hand—whether it's A-K or something else—you want to get your opponent committed to the pot. If you have A-K and the flop comes K-Q, you're a little afraid of it, but you still bet it. You realize that if somebody plays back at you, you're still trying to catch a card, unless your opponent is a weak player. If the flop comes K-Q, your opponent might be holding K-Q or J-10. It's even possible that he might call you with A-10, hoping to catch the gutshot straight on the turn. And sorry to say, that happens more often than it should!

PLAYING BIG PAIRS

The three hands that knock more people out of pot-limit tournaments than any other ones are Q-Q, J-J and A-K. Suppose you have Q-Q. The flop comes K-7-4.

YOU

FLOP

When you have Q-Q and the flop comes with either a king or an ace, I think that you should be ready to give it up. If you are going to win the pot (with the king or ace on the board), you want to win it in a showdown; you don't want to put any money in the pot.

If you're against only one opponent with your pair of queens and the flop comes something like K-7-4, Tom will bet the pot in an attempt to win it right there. If his opponent has a king in his hand, obviously he won't be successful, but at least he hasn't given the man a chance to hit an ace, in case he has one in the hole with a card other than a king (an A-J or A-Q, for example). I wouldn't make a play at this pot myself, but that is the difference in our approaches.

My thinking is that if I have raised preflop, it is likely that my opponents will have the overcard if it comes on the flop. The idea of betting to find out where you are in the hand just doesn't make sense to me in this situation, whether the pot is multiway or two-handed. My theory is that if my opponent bets on the flop, I can make a decision about whether he has a hand—but if I bet into him, I take the chance of getting raised. If my hand is the best one on the flop, there is a good chance that another overcard is not going to come out. Now, I have my information without losing any money.

You can bet the hand on fourth street, if you want to, or you can play it to show it down. There's already enough in the pot so that you can win some real money: Why bet it again?

Suppose you are in front position with the pair of queens, you check, and your opponent bets. Ask yourself, "Who am I playing this pot against? Is my opponent a guy who would bet an underpair, or would he need top pair to bet?" Since you have played with him for a while, you should know the answer. I believe that you will make more money in this situation by checking than you will ever make by leading because you can get yourself in a trap by betting the hand. Now, suppose you check and your opponent also checks. You pretty well know that you have the best hand, because if he wanted to trap you in this situation, he would be trapping you with a big hand. If he had a king with a decent kicker, he would bet it. But if he flopped a set, he would let you come to him because you were the original aggressor.

Suppose my opponent is sitting in front of me. The flop again comes K-rag-rag, and he checks it to me. Whether I would bet with Q-Q in this situation depends on what I know about my opponent. If an aggressive player checks to me, I probably would bet it, but I still am not going to get broke to this hand, no matter what.

What happens if you bet the queens and get called? Even though you've made the bet, you can still shut down. Your opponent might be holding K-rag in the big blind, for example, and although he wouldn't bet the hand, he might call you with it. You never know what some players will call a raise with from the big blind, especially when you're playing short-handed in a tournament.

When the action narrows down to four or five players in a tournament, a player might call a raise with a rag ace or a rag king. Many times, players will even call with hands such as K-5 suited, "The Broke's Lament." Of course, *you* are not going to play that way, but some other players do.

HITTING A SET ON THE FLOP

When you hit your set of queens on the flop, how you play the hand depends on how many players have called your raise before the flop. Say that you raised and three players called. In this case, you can lead with the hand and just pray that somebody plays back at you. If there are a couple of connectors on the flop, especially if they are suited, you have all the more reason to bet the pot. And if you are playing against super aggressive players, you definitely want to bet because they often will bluff at you, or will call with an underpair. You want to get these types of players to commit money to the pot as soon as possible. After all, three queens is a big hand.

Say that you raised the pot before the flop, nobody reraised, and the flop comes:

YOU

FLOP

How do you play the hand? You are still the favorite to win the pot, although in smaller pot-limit games, you might also run into a player holding J-10. Still, I would lead at the pot, hoping that someone with A-K has flopped top two pair. You can't be afraid to bet, always thinking that the nut hand is out against you.

WHEN YOU FLOP AN OVERPAIR

Suppose you are holding Q-Q in a raised pot with two callers, the flop comes with suited cards, and you are *not* holding the queen of that suit.

YOU

FLOP

What's your best play? If I am the first to act with only two opponents, there's a good chance that my queens are the best hand, unless someone has flopped a lucky flush. A more likely hand for an opponent to be holding is a hand such as the A♣ J♥ with a draw to the nut flush. With only two opponents, I am going to lead at the pot. However, against four opponents, my queens are much more vulnerable. If I am first to act, I will just check with my overpair. If I am last to act, I will bet.

Say that you have an opponent who never reraises with A-K. Of course, that's not such a bad play since you can get yourself into a trap with A-K, as we've already discussed. Again, the flop comes J♣ 8♣ 2♣. What do you do in this situation? You don't know whether your opponent has A-K, but it is a likely hand for him to be holding. He could even have the A♣ K♦, making you an underdog in the hand. In that case, he would have 28 outs, including nine clubs, three aces (if he has the ace of clubs), and two kings, making his hand about even-money.

How you play the hand against this opponent goes back to how well you know your opponents—the most important skill in big-bet poker.

Now, let's take a look at a different scenario. Suppose you're the one holding the A♣ and the flop comes suited in clubs:

YOU

FLOP

As for me, I would never call a bet with this hand on this flop. And I do mean *never*. In pot-limit and no-limit, when I have two of a suit in my hand and two of my suit come on the flop, it always seems to me that I have a better chance of making the hand than when the flop comes suited and I have only one of that suit.

Of course, the odds are exactly the same in either situation, but still, I don't draw for the fourth suited to come on the board. How will I get any action, anyway, if the fourth suited card comes on the board? But when I have two of the suit in my hand and a third suited card falls on the board, I may get action when I bet the flush.

BUILDING THE POT ON THE FLOP WITH POCKET ACES

Obviously, pocket aces is the best hand that you can start with in any high hold'em game. The only time that I would ever limp before the flop with aces is in a very aggressive game. Why? Because in an aggressive game when you limp with aces, one guy might raise, then this one calls, that one calls—and then you can turn the aces into a powerhouse by coming over the top of them. You can eliminate a lot of players that way, and if you get called, you still know that you have the best hand going in. After that, it's just Lady Luck's call from the flop onward.

Another way of playing aces is to bring them in for a raise and hope that someone reraises you. If someone does reraise, just flat call the reraise if you're playing against only one opponent. Then if the board comes with rags, you're in good shape. The only time that you should be afraid is when the board comes with kings, queens or jacks because your opponent could have been raising with pocket pairs of these ranks and has flopped a set. If the flop comes K-Q-J, you can dump the aces in a flash if your opponent comes out swinging at you, without anyone knowing that you held them (since you only flat called the raise). But when the flop is a split board, you can trap a single opponent really good because you didn't shut him out before the flop.

If you're playing in a normal game, you usually bring it in for a raise with pocket aces because, although you want to make money with them, you don't want to have seven people drawing at your aces. Even though the aces are still the favorite, they are not a big favorite with that many people in the pot. The worst scenario when you hold pocket aces is this: Say that you're playing in a $10/$10 game and you can only raise $40 from the first seat with your aces, and you get six callers—all of whom have pocket pairs. This could happen!

In fact, I played a pot once in Dallas when the flop came with the Q♦ 10♦ 5♦. One player made the nut flush and the other three each flopped a set. The turn and river came with a running pair of fours and the queens-full won the pot. The worst player in the hand was able to get away from the three tens because of the amount of money being moved at the pot. Any broken board in the world can come and make a set for an opponent when you have pocket aces, but you know that coming in. And that's why I suggest raising before the flop to limit the number of your opponents.

Suppose you're are holding A-A and the flop comes:

YOU

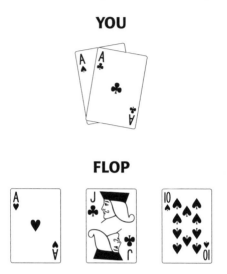

FLOP

How do you play trip aces in this situation? I like to lead with the aces in this situation. The only thing that I'm worried about is the K-Q, and even then I'm not dead. What you don't want to do is let people draw at you for free, because if a king or a queen slip off the deck, it is very possible that someone will make a straight. So, you want to take the lead against this dangerous flop. If you are raised, you probably will want to move in on the raiser. Anybody, including me, might get broke with this hand in this situation!

The perfect flop, the one that you want to see when you have pocket aces, is A-K-rag, A-Q-rag, or A-J-rag. Somebody might be holding any two of the top cards and make two pair on the flop. Oh boy, do I like to lead with this type of flop! I want my opponent to have an ace in his hand because he can't give any action unless he has an ace or has flopped a set. You also want to lead at the pot because you don't want to give an opponent with high connectors the chance to make a belly-buster straight on the turn.

However, I never lead at the pot with that thought in mind. I lead at the pot thinking, "Oh, baby, I know he's flopped two pair and he's going to play back at me!"

Now, suppose the same type of flop comes, except that two of the cards are suited.

YOU

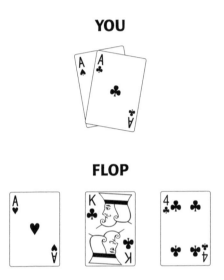

FLOP

What's your play? This is another flop that you want to lead at with pocket aces, because you want your opponents to play back at you. If they make their flush or straight on the turn, so what? You're still drawing to a full house with your three aces.

Leading at the pot in pot-limit or no-limit always makes sense because, if your opponents hit the flop with two pair, they can't get away from it and you can build a giant pot for yourself, especially if they raise when you bet. That's when you know that you have them by the throat because they've made a substantial commitment to the pot—and they will have to make a straight or a flush to beat you if they have drawing hands.

Suppose you check, your opponent bets, and then you raise. Often, he will lay down his hand, because you're tipping off the strength of your hand. But if you lead at the pot, the ordinary player will seldom give you credit for having the nuts.

Say that the flop comes:

YOU

FLOP

You're sitting in last position, and a player leads at the pot. Now what do you do with your trip aces?

It all depends. I am a risk taker, and I like to win big pots, so I may just smooth call him on the flop and wait until fourth street to make my move. Of course, you can lose the pot if the wrong card comes off.

PLAYING DRAWS

What's the use in playing a draw if you can't get it paid off when you make it? That is the fallacy in playing draws in pot-limit and no-limit hold'em. Against a top player, if the flop comes with two of a suit and you call a bet, and then if the third card to your suit comes on the turn and you bet your flush, the top player won't pay you off. You are a 4.5 to 1 underdog to make the draw with one card to come, and if you are successful in making your hand, you aren't going to win any more money with it anyway.

So, if you decide to make the draw, the only way to play it is to put in a pot-sized bet to get enough money into the pot to make it worth your while to draw to it. Making such a draw makes sense only if you do it against weaker players, because they will pay you off on the end. Straight draws can be harder for your opponents to read than flush draws, so you might prefer drawing to a straight than drawing to a flush.

WHAT ABOUT J-10?

I rate a hand such as J-10 suited as a better hand than K-10 suited in a multiway pot because the J-10 gives you more straight possibilities. Your kicker also makes it easier to get away from the hand if you flop top pair. For example, if the flop comes 10-7-2, your kicker is only a jack, whereas with the K-10, your kicker is the second-highest one that you can have.

YOU

FLOP

In this situation, you could fold your top pair/jack kicker to action on the flop, depending on who the action came from, whereas you wouldn't necessarily need to fold a K-10 since you have top pair with a good kicker and an overcard to the flop. In a multiway unraised pot, a better flop for J-10 might look similar to this one:

YOU

FLOP

Suppose you're in late position and four players see the flop for the minimum bet. You have top pair and an open-ended straight draw, so you have a good chance at either having the best hand on the flop, or improving to a straight. Just don't get too heavily involved in the action since you have no kicker. If you keep the pot small, you can go with this hand. Therefore, if you can get free cards, take them.

Remember that making draws in pot-limit hold'em can be dangerous and expensive. With these board cards, you can catch any queen or any 7 to make the straight, but at what price? What happens if you don't improve to a straight on fourth street? If you're first to act and check, your opponent may fire at you with a pot-sized bet so big it wouldn't be poker to call. You want a cheap shot at making your draw to a better hand on the turn.

Further, what if somebody already has J-Q? In pot-limit hold'em, you have to use your head. Think through all these things before you decide how to play the hand.

PLAYING BOTTOM TWO PAIR

In a pot-limit hold'em cash game that I played a few years ago, five players were in for $40 each. I was on the button with the Q♥ J♥ and was getting big odds for my money, so I called. Here came the flop:

T.J.

FLOP

It was pass, pass, bet, before it got to me. I raised with top pair, an overcard, and a flush draw. Joe Blow from Idaho beat me into the pot with his call. The board ragged off on fourth street. I had begun the hand with $850 and I had around $300 left; I wasn't going to dog the hand at that point so I came at it again.

On the river, I missed everything—I still just had top pair. Joe won the hand with 8-7 offsuit. On the flop, my hand was favored over 8-7 offsuit, the bottom two pair, but my opponent lucked out when I didn't improve. Like the commercials say, don't try this play at home.

Don't count on winning any pot-limit hold'em pot with bottom two pair. In both pot-limit and no-limit hold'em, it's a treacherous hand. A lot of players forget that there is such a thing as a running pair. For example, the board could have come with a 4 on the turn and another 4 on the river. Take a look:

T.J.   **JOE**

BOARD

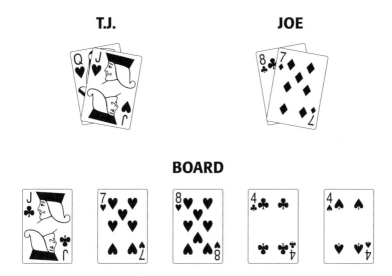

Now how do things look for the 8-7? Joe has made eights over sevens, while I've come out smelling like a rose with jacks over fours.

You need to protect your hand when you flop bottom two pair. Do whatever you can do to win it on the flop. I had multiple ways to win the pot—nine hearts, two jacks, and three queens times two (two draws)—plus the possibility of a running pair. That's 32 ways to make the hand. I definitely had the edge over my opponent.

And I was doing the betting, which gave me even more of an edge. You might lose the pot (as I did), but you still should always get your money in correctly. A lot of times, you might win the pot right on the flop with your bet. And even if your opponent double pairs and calls or raises your bet, you're still a slight favorite with two cards to come.

When you flop bottom two pair, there are times when it might be correct for you to continue with the hand. In the example above, suppose the pot has been raised before the flop. Since Joe already has put in a lot of money, it becomes correct for him to keep playing the hand, just as it is correct for the player with top pair/top kicker to continue. Even if Joe is a slight dog, he isn't much more of a dog than the other hand. Many times, then, it is correct for both players to go to the center.

Here is an amendment to this story. When the game started, I had $1,000 and when this hand came up, I had $850 that I was jeopardizing in the play of this hand. But if you had $5,000 in front of you, or even $3,000, you might play the hand differently. With a big bankroll, you might trail all the way with this hand; that is, check. If you don't hit on fourth street, and your opponent is an aggressive player, he will put the test to you. Then, what are you going to do? You only have one card to come to hit the hand; one-half of your outs are gone. You fold.

But with a short amount of money in a raised pot such as this one, the gamble is well worth it. You see, when you have more money, you have more reason to protect your stack, especially in a tournament. With less money, you might be more likely to gamble because your risk is limited.

In a tournament, in fact, I would never make the play that I did, because it isn't smart to jeopardize your whole stack in an even-money situation. Also, you wouldn't be playing the Q♥ J♥ in a tournament; you wouldn't even call the original bet with it. Tom suggests, however, that he would play the hand in a rebuy tournament, or in the early stages of any tournament, if he is on the button with it and only has to call a small bet with the hand.

So there are at least two ways of looking at this situation.

The situation changes depending upon the circumstances. For example, at a four-handed table in a tournament, you might play the hand aggressively against the J♣ 7♥ 8♥ flop. Four-handed, you don't necessarily need to have a big hand or a big flop. In short-handed tournament action, people frequently attack the blinds, and they don't need big hands to do that. If I flop top pair and a flush draw against one opponent (who doesn't have to have a big hand to be in the pot), I very likely will come over the top of him right on the flop. So, if you play this hand short-handed in a tournament, you either play it aggressively from the flop onward, or you don't play it at all.

When can you play Q-J suited in a raised pot in a tournament? When the opening raise is small, you have a lot of chips in front of you, you're playing short-handed, and you're trying to knock your opponent out of the tournament. When you make your original call, you're not thinking, "I have the best hand with a queen high." Many times, you know that you don't have the best hand going in, but you have a hand that has some potential. With the huge implied odds in pot-limit, remember that you don't have to start with the best hand all of the time. It all depends on whether you believe that you can outplay your opponent, or that you will be paid off if you hit your hand. If you flop the top-pair/flush-draw, play it aggressively, the way I played the hand with short money.

Obviously, the number of players at your table has a lot of impact on the hands that you play in a tournament. Most tournaments today start with a ten-handed table, but we used to start with eleven players in Dallas—and believe me, it takes a much bigger hand to win an eleven-handed game than it does to win a four-handed game. This applies even more to ring games than to tournaments. The optimal field for a pot-limit or no-limit game or tournament table is eight-handed.

Why?

Because you have a lot more maneuverability in the plays that you can make, and in the hands you select to play.

The more people in the game, the bigger the hand it takes to win; the fewer people, the smaller the hand it takes to win.

Full-handed, you have to give more respect to your opponents. Short-handed, things get down to the nuts and bolts of the game. And that is when you find out what kind of player you are, especially in tournaments.

In other words, your play changes dramatically depending upon the number of people in the game. You have to be more cognizant of the quality of your hands in a full ring game, whereas in short-handed play, you need to be more cognizant of the quality of your opponents. A lot of players have the skill to *get to* the final table, but there are very few who have the skill to *play* the final table.

Over the years, Tom and I have been approached hundreds of times by players who ask us, "What am I doing wrong? I get there, but I never win."

The bottom line is that they haven't honed their short-handed skills well enough. Here is where people falter: They don't understand the value of their hands, as hand values change dramatically in short-handed play. And they don't seize situations properly.

In tournaments, it's *carpe diem*. "Seize the day." You have to take advantage of situations and opportunities to win a tournament.

Now let's move on to playing the turn in pot-limit hold'em. That's when things really heat up!

HOW TO TURN ON THE STEAM ON THE TURN IN POT-LIMIT

On the turn in pot-limit hold'em, you still want to build the pot if you have a hand. And again, I suggest that you always bet the size of the pot because you never want to tip off your opponents about the value of your hand. If I have a made hand, I usually will still lead at the pot, unless I'm playing against a loose-goose who gives a lot of action. In that case, I may check the hand and let him come at me.

Against a loose player, Tom says that he may change the size of his bet; he'll bet only three-quarters of the pot, for example. That approach also has some value. But suppose five good players are in the game and four not-so-good players. When you're in a pot with the five good players, are you going to make a full bet, but when you're in it with the four other players, are you going to make a lesser bet? I believe that if you reduce your bet size with some of them, you have to do it with all of them, or else you're going to tip the value of your hand. And I never want to tip the strength of my hand one iota.

Of course, Tom is talking about varying his bet size in a head-up situation against a loose player. But remember that the other players are still sitting in the game—and you're going to be playing hands with those other guys, too. What are you going to do, tip them off that when you underbet the pot, you have a big hand, and when you bet the size of the pot, you don't? I don't believe that you should do that because the underbet that you make in the hand against a loose opponent is only one hand among many hands that you're going to be playing. I don't want to give the good players a tell that I underbet the pot when I have a hand, unless I'm trying to put a reverse tell on them.

What I'm looking at is the big picture of the game. One hand is only a small part of the puzzle and I don't want to give away any pieces of the puzzle by the way that I play one hand, because the good players will pick up on it. Good players pick up on everything!

Think of the big picture all the time while you are playing.

PLAYING A DRAWING HAND

Now suppose you have a draw. On the flop, you might want to bet your draw because you have two chances to win: They might throw their hands away, or you might catch your card on the turn and make a big hand. On fourth street, however, I would not bet the draw. The main thing to realize about drawing hands is that you must be in position to play them.

Suppose you're in early position with a draw on the flop, and it doesn't get there on the turn. Can you lead at this hand again? No, you cannot. Your opponents are going to detect that you're on a drawing hand and they're going to try to take the pot away from you. But if you're in position on a drawing hand—the other guys are in front of you—then you can bet your draw. In other words, the only time you can bet a draw is when you are sitting *behind* the other players and they check to you on the flop. On fourth street, they still have to act first.

By betting the draw on the flop, if they check to you on fourth street, then you can also check and get a free card.

This strategy is similar to limit hold'em except that in limit play, you have to raise to get that free card, whereas in pot-limit, you can simply play position to get a free card. In pot-limit and no-limit when you're in late position and you're on a draw, one of the worst things that you can do is bet on fourth street with one card to come after everybody has checked to you.

Why?

Because you could have gotten the draw for free, nada, zilch!

Further, if you bet on the turn, you're opening it up for them to raise and shut you out of making your draw. I don't mind making the bet on the flop and opening it to a raise because I still have two cards to come, and I can decide whether I want to play the draw or fold right there.

Also, I'm not saying that you always have to bet your draw on the flop from a late position. Sometimes, you might decide to just check. But remember, what's the use of making a drawing hand and not winning any money with it? There's also the deception factor when you bet your draw on the flop. Your opponents can't be sure about what type of hand you have and they may not guess that you're on a draw, so you may win the pot right there. In pot-limit, I believe that your options are better when you bet the draw than when you don't bet it.

THE CARDINAL SIN

If you bet a draw in early position and don't make it on the turn, you're throwing up a white flag. You can't bet it on fourth street when it doesn't get there. Why? Because if you do bet it, you're committing a lot of money with only one card to come.

You also might get raised, and then what? The cardinal sin in pot-limit is betting that draw *again* on fourth street, opening yourself up to a raise. In fact, some of the good players might put you on a draw and raise with nothing just to shut you out of the pot!

So, you can bet your draw on the flop from a late position when you're last to act, but not from a front spot. When you're in late position, if an opponent appears to have made something on the turn and bets into you, you can always get away from the hand if you haven't made it yet. Plus, you might have made a big hand, in which case you may want to check it along on fourth street. Then you can let them come at you on fifth street, where you can put a raise on them. Being in that late position gives you lots of options.

Now let's take a look at bluffing in pot-limit hold'em: when you can, how you can, and why you should or shouldn't.

BLUFFING: WHO, WHEN, HOW

Nobody can bluff a weak player—if you know nothing else about bluffing, this one thing will get you through. Trying to bluff a calling station would be like attempting to commit suicide. These players are likely to call you with the worst possible hands, ones that you can only imagine in your worst poker nightmares. All they know about is what they have: They never think about what anybody else is holding. And yes, some of them take a swing at pot-limit hold'em, probably because they've heard it's a great action game. They're right.

There are exceptions to every rule, of course, so you can occasionally bluff a weak player. The situation has to be just right, though. Say that you're in a tournament with a lot of chips and he doesn't have very many chips. If you bluff at this player, you have put it to him that if he calls and is wrong in making the call, he is out of the tournament. Your bet says, "You'd better be right, because if you're wrong you're out of action." This type of bluff is used a lot by strong players because they know that it is very hard for even a calling station to make the call under these circumstances. They may have been calling all along, but when it jeopardizes all of their chips, they suddenly get scared.

However, I never try this type of bluff against a good player. Why? Because a strong player will pick it off in a New York minute. For example, in 1986 at the World Series of Poker deep into the tournament (the third day of the championship no-limit hold'em event), the action was passed to Berry Johnston who held K-8 on the button. He brought it in for a raise, trying to pick up the blinds. Tommy Grimes had an A-Q in the big blind and came over the top of him. But Berry had one-half of his chips in the pot and decided that he wasn't going to give it up. He caught an 8 to win the pot. And then he went on to win the championship. This was the key hand for him.

The point is that you just don't mess with a top player unless you've got the goods.

The Big Bluff

The best bluff is the big bluff. When somebody is trying to take a shot at you, you come back over the top of him. This is the resteal, or the rebluff. You can try to resteal when you think that a player is out of line. Maybe he's been bringing in a lot of pots for raises, and he doesn't always have premium hands when he does it. So now, you might decide to gamble with that A-J that you might have mucked against a solid player's raise from early position.

You can also make a strong rebluff by waiting until later in the hand. For example, you might not even hold a pair, but you know from the way the action is taking place that the raiser is swinging at the pot. You might try to take it away from him on fourth or fifth street, rather than on the flop, because you want a little bit of money in the pot to make it worth your while.

I once tried a resteal in a limit hold'em tournament when I knew that my opponent was out of line. I brought it in for a raise with the K♠ J♠. The flop came:

T.J.

BOARD

I had two overcards and a flush draw on the flop. The big blind check-raised me on the turn when a blank came off. He could have had a variety of hands, but I flat called him. On fifth street, the board paired with nines. The big blind checked to me, I bet, and he raised. Although I had missed everything and only had two overcards, I came back over the top of him again. He mucked his hand.

Once in a while, in pot-limit or no-limit ring games as well as in tournaments, you can make this play when you put a guy on a weak hand, because there is enough money in the pot so that you can really send it to him. In almost every tournament

I've won, I have made at least one grandstand play. Luckily, I have been right about 95 percent of the time. Just because I am the type of player who likes to lead in pot-limit hold'em doesn't mean than everybody does. A lot of players don't like to do that.

PLAYING THE RIVER, OVER AND OUT!

The last subject we need to cover before it's over and out with pot-limit hold'em is how to play on the river. Suppose you're playing in a multiway pot on the river. If you have two or three opponents, it is probable that at least one of them has a drawing hand. Suppose you're in late position and a scare card comes on the river that looks as though it might complete a drawing hand. I suggest just turning over your cards without a bet if the action is checked to you, even if you have top set. In other words, be careful about betting if a scare card comes on the river.

What if a scare card doesn't come on the river? In that case, I will bet if I think that I have the best hand, even if it's only top pair with top kicker. Sometimes, a player will try to trap me on the river, but he usually will have sprung his trap earlier than the river card (though not always). If someone has put me on a draw, he usually will make his play on fourth street because he doesn't want me to be drawing. Therefore, I am less worried about a trap on the river when a blank comes than I am when a scare card comes. And that's why I'll usually value bet if I think that I have the best hand.

If I bet on the river when a blank comes off and then somebody raises me, I will have to reevaluate my hand. It becomes a question of judgment, based on what I know about the player. Or my decision may be based on my chip position if I'm playing a tournament. The strength of my hand also influences my decision. One-pair hands that are check-raised on the river usually are very vulnerable, though not always. It depends somewhat on your opponent, and whether you think he is somebody who's capable of taking a shot at you.

Trust Your Instincts

Of course, certain players will try to win a hand from you on the river with a stone bluff. But if you've been observant, you probably know who they are—and part of that depends on how things come up, how the hand is played. If you've been playing poker for a while, you know that your first instincts have been correct up to 98 percent of the time. Those instincts cannot be taught; they come from thousands of hours of playing. Whenever you make a play that goes against your instincts, you're usually wrong. You end up trying to figure out some way in which a different scenario could come up. In essence, you start talking yourself out of something.

It's like the guy who calls on the end: He figures out a hand that he can beat, and then he puts his opponent on that hand—not the hand the man has, but a hand that he can beat so he can justify calling the bet. People do this all the time. In limit hold'em, it's the worst thing in the world to do, because at the end of the day, the bets that you save on the end probably will add up to what you win for the day. If you can win three or more bets an hour in limit poker, that's a pretty nice deal. But in pot-limit and no-limit, you're looking to win a lot more than that.

If you get stuck in pot-limit and no-limit hold'em, especially no-limit, you can get even on one hand if you have a bankroll. You can be $5,000 stuck, put $10,000 in the pot, win one hand, and suddenly you're a $5,000 winner. In pot-limit, if you use the strategy that we have been talking about—maximizing the pot—you can get even quickly. You can even come from behind to win.

WHAT MAKES A GREAT BIG-BET POKER PLAYER?

In addition to having judgment and experience, the players who can maximize the pot in pot-limit and no-limit hold'em are the better players—that's what makes them better. When it comes down to the end where you have to decide whether to bet the hand or check it, the better player will *know* whether he has the best hand. In fact, he'll get a bet out of it in situations where the lesser player will not.

Theoretically, the cards break even in the long run, even though fluctuations happen in the short run, and over a lifetime, some players will be slightly luckier than others. But I maintain that the top player not only will beat you with *his* cards, he will beat you with *your* cards. He will win more with your cards than you will, and he will lose less with them.

Poker, especially tournament poker, is a game of mistakes.

# **16** WRAPPING IT UP

Tom and I realize that there is more than one way to play no-limit hold'em. You definitely can win no-limit tournaments playing the strategy we explore and advise in this book. You can also win by using a different approach. One of them is called "small ball," a strategy that aims at keeping the pot small and allowing you to play small cards.

PLAYING SMALL BALL TO MANAGE THE SIZE OF A POT

We've all played "small ball" to start off a tournament. It means that unless you have the stone nuts, you don't create huge pots. You want to win smaller pots and have them build up in your stack. That's small ball, and it's a viable approach. It's pretty much what you do in multiday tournaments as a regular part of your play.

However, in the early part of a tournament, I don't play small ball when I'm the raiser, like some of the other pros do. I also don't play as many pots in the first couple of days as a lot of players do. As the tournament progresses, I start playing more and more hands.

PLAYING BIG BALL
TO BUILD A POT

Most players raise three to four times the size of the blinds for their first raise. I raise five to six times the big blind, strictly because I don't play that many pots—but when I'm the initial raiser, I usually want to play a big pot. I think I have the best hand or I wouldn't be raising. I'm putting my money in with pretty strong hands early in the tournament. And of course, I start building a bigger pot by raising bigger before the flop. That way, I can bet more on the flop since there's more money in the pot. And more again on the turn and river. That's not small ball—that's big ball! The whole idea is that I can win five pots whereas you might have to win fifteen pots to accumulate the same amount of money that I win in five pots.

I like everybody thinking that I'm playing real tight, because I can take advantage of a lot of situations that way. When somebody describes my play as tight-aggressive, they're probably right. Actually, I am every type of player that you can think of at some time in a tournament. Solid or tight or aggressive or semi-aggressive or passive or just a regular player who plays in the middle of the stream—I play all those styles at some different point in the tournament. I don't want to get pigeonholed, to let anybody think that I just play one way and they can run over me, because they can't. Sure, there are times when I play small ball, but that's not my usual style at all.

DANIEL NEGREANU
AND SMALL BALL

Daniel Negreanu has written a lot about small ball. He plays those little connectors around the back, as long as nobody raises too much, and looks to hit one often enough to make the gamble worthwhile. Obviously, you don't want to play just one opponent with those hands too often; you want to play multiway pots. When he's hitting with some of those hands, Daniel will play anybody, he'll stand raises around back and come in with small pairs and little connectors.

If you're famous for doing that as a small-ball player, a lot of people will recognize how you play, so they're not going to get crazy playing pots with you. Suppose you've called a raise from around back and the flop comes something like 4-7-8. People understand the small-ball approach these days, so when a small connecting flop comes out, they are far more likely to expect that someone is playing a 5-6, especially if that player is known for playing small ball. The point is that if you're alert and aware of who you're playing against, you can see the possibility that players like Daniel might've hit their hand. So, you have to slow down a little bit until he proves that he didn't hit it. (When Daniel plays those small hands, they're always connected, there's no air between them. They're not cards like 6-8 and they're definitely not 6-9.)

What if flops don't run in the small-ball direction? The small-ball player might call those little raises twenty times and burn up a lot of money before he can ever hit enough flops to win a pot with them. So, it's just a matter of what you're willing to do. I've called with those small connectors. I try not to play them in the blinds because I have to act first after the flop, but if I'm in the highjack seat or the cutoff or the button, that's a different ballgame. If it's a multiway pot, I'll come in and take a flop to those kinds of hands. But I don't make a habit of it. I'm not going to burn up a bunch of chips that I can use later in the tournament when I have a hand that I can double or triple or quadruple up with. If those chips are no longer in your stack because you've spent them on little cards, you can't do that.

MAKE THE SIZE OF YOUR RAISES CONSISTENT

I realize that small-ball players want to raise something like two and a half times the big blind instead of three times the blind. But you've got to understand that a lot of players these days are sharp, they understand no-limit hold'em very well. So if you're coming in for a raise that is five times the blind one time, and three times the blinds the next time, these sharp players are watching, noticing what kinds of hands you're showing down in pots. And before long, they can pick off what type of hand you're playing based on how money you're betting. That's why I say that if you raise three to four times the blind, do it consistently. If you raise five to six times the blind, do it consistently. That way, you don't tip off the strength of your hand.

Say that you're playing $25/$50 and a player makes it $200. Then on his next raise, he makes it $150. That's a signal that he's playing a small hand. He risks having an opponent come right over the top of him. If you want to make a two-and-a-half-times raise to keep the pot small, that's fine. Just be sure do it every single time.

HAS SMALL BALL CHANGED TOURNAMENT PLAY?

I've heard people say that this small-ball approach is one of the ways that no-limit hold'em has changed, but I just don't see the big changes that everybody talks about. I don't think the basic game has changed primarily because of one big factor: When you're playing in a tournament, the only thing that you've ever been able to control is the table you are playing at.

The only thing that I guarantee has changed is that some of these "new kids on the block" have played more hands than I have—and I've been playing poker for fifty years—because they've played so many hours online. More people understand the basics of the game these days than ever used to. Many of them still have to get accustomed to looking you in the eye instead of looking at a machine, but when it comes to knowing the basic parts of the game, they know them. And that's why so many of them make their way to Las Vegas to play the World Series of Poker.

ALL ROADS LEAD TO LAS VEGAS

In ancient times, the saying was "All roads lead to Rome." In the world of tournament poker, all roads lead to the Las Vegas. Winning a bracelet at the Series is the goal of every serious tournament player, I can tell you that for sure. After you've won your first bracelet, you want to win one for your other wrist. And then you want to feel the high again, so you aim for winning another one. The good news is that every year, you get another chance to compete against the best poker players in the world at the most prestigious tournament in all of poker. And when you come out on top, you feel like a million dollars, whether you win that much or not. You see, it's not just the money, it's the winning that counts the most.

I've been on the road playing poker for four decades. In the old days I played in a lot of smoky backrooms, driving across the dusty back roads of Texas and the South to make my living at poker. These days I'm still on the road, but it's a lot easier. I can fly to the East coast for a big tournament, get back home for a few weeks, and then fly to Vegas or Mississippi or Aruba for the next one.

And I'll tell another thing that makes it easier these days. You don't have to learn to play poker by the seat of your pants like we did in the old days. You can learn it by studying books, practicing in little tournaments in clean and safe casinos, and playing a million-plus hands in online cardrooms. And boy, does that save time and money!

Tom and I wrote this book to save you from a lot of the work we had to do just to get up to speed on the game. We hope that with our help, you'll be able to shift your game into high gear so we can shake hands in the winners' circle at the end of the tournament road, the World Series of Poker.

HOW I WON THE CHAMPION OF CHAMPIONS TOURNAMENT

Tom McEvoy

As one of the twenty-five living Main Event champions, I was invited to compete for the title of Champion of Champions in a special tournament at the 2009 World Series of Poker designed to celebrate its 40th anniversary. The Rio in Las Vegas, host of the annual WSOP, put up a unique prize package for the winner: a vintage, fully restored, bright cherry red, 1970 Corvette convertible. In addition, the champion received the first ever Binion Cup, named for the Binion family, which founded the World Series of Poker in 1970. Jack Binion, son of WSOP founder Benny Binion, presented the cup to the winner—none other than me!

Playing against the cream of the crop was exhilarating, to say the least. As we began play on the first of two days with twenty of the twenty-five living champions in action, you could feel the electricity in the air. Several of us were wearing Stetsons for an historic photo that reminded me of the early tournaments that were dominated by players from Texas. Believe me, each of us really wanted to win this tournament—for the cup, the car, and of course, the bragging rights that come with winning the title of Champion of Champions.

I cannot remember facing a tougher line-up in my entire thirty-year poker career. In the grand tradition of the World

Series of Poker, which started out as a winner-take-all tournament with $10,000 in chips, the Champion of Champions event followed suit. The opening blinds were $25/$50 with one hour rounds. We battled for almost six hours the first day, finally getting down to the final ten when the blinds were $200/$400 with a $25 ante.

THE FINAL TEN

Jamie Gold, the 2006 champion, had the unfortunate distinction of going broke very early in the first level of play. Then, one by one, the remaining players were eliminated until we got down to one final table of ten. Phil Hellmuth was determined to make the TV table, and after 2005 champion Joe Hachem went broke with slightly more chips than Phil, the "Poker Brat" got his wish, albeit with fewer than $1,500 in chips. When we came back to play the next day, we were greeted by the TV cameras set up by ESPN.

Doyle Brunson was in a humorous mood when we started our final day. He told Phil that he had confirmed what Doyle had known all along—Phil would do anything to make the TV table. Then Doyle asked, "Where are all the Internet players? Oh, there he is." He was referring to Peter Eastgate, the youngest player at the table and the reigning World Champion of Poker.

As luck would have it, Phil, by far the shortest stack, drew the big blind the very first hand. Carlos Mortensen, who busted Phil when he won the 2001 championship, did it again by raising on the first hand dealt, putting Phil all-in if he chose to call. Everyone passed to Phil, who hemmed and hawed for a minute before sayin, "Heck, I'll have to call with practically any two cards."

And he did—with a suited 10-5. Surprisingly, Phil was not in that bad a shape as he held two overcards against Carlos' pocket deuces. Alas, poker's famous brat did not improve. Phil was very gracious as he left the table in defeat, shaking everyone's hand and wishing us all good luck.

Peter Eastgate went out a few hands later. He raised preflop with the 8♠ 7♠ and 1995 champion Dan Harrington reraised. Peter thought about it for awhile before making a play that I definitely would not have made against "Action Dan." He pushed all-in. In my opinion, Dan would not have reraised this early at the final table without a big hand, so this was definitely not the time to make that kind of move. With a touch of humor, Dan said, "Well everybody has to take a stand sometime," and then called—with pocket aces. He also remarked that he wished his aces had been up against a different type of hand before the flop. His analysis proved right when the flop came down 8-6-5. Peter flopped a pair with an open-ended straight draw and two cards to come. Yikes! Dan sweated it out, but Peter got no help and hit the rail in 9th place.

The tournament took a long time to finish, finally ending around 1:00 am in the 12th round of play with the blinds at $1,000/$2,000 and a $300 ante. Along the way I eliminated Doyle in 8th place. The 1986 champion Berry Johnston, short-stacked to begin with, finally went broke to Carlos, soon followed by 1996 champion Huck Seed.

I was fortunate to win a few pots early against Carlos, knocking his stack down considerably and becoming co-chip leader with Harrington. But when Carlos made top two pair against 1993 champion Jim Bechtel's flopped set, our opening chip leader went out in 5th place. Down to four players now, Robert Varkoni, the 2002 Champion, was the shortest stack.

Getting Lucky in Three-Way Action

In an interesting three-way hand, Robert raised the pot to $3,000 preflop, and I reraised to $9,000 on the button with A-K offsuit. Bechtel then pushed in for about $34,000 from the big blind. Varkoni quickly folded, leaving it up to me. I finally decided to make the call, but soon realized that sometimes you make the wrong play at the right time and get lucky. Jim had pocket kings and Robert said he had folded a suited ace—oops, I was in worse shape than I thought. However, I admit that the poker gods smiled on me flopping one of the two remaining aces in the deck. My hand held up to give me over $100,000 of the $200,000 chips in play. I remained in the lead the rest of the way, but Harrington and Varkoni were only one double-up from taking it away from me.

We played three-handed for almost three hours before I broke Dan Harrington with the K♦ Q♦ versus his 9-9. I called his all-in bet on an A-Q-X flop, hoping he didn't have an ace. I was right and my pair of queens held up to send Dan home in 3rd place.

Shooting it Out Against a Longshot

If players were betting on Varkoni's chances of making it heads-up against me at the final table, it would have been a very long shot indeed. But what our colleagues didn't fully realize was our mindset. As I told the ESPN crew in my pre-tournament interview, "Nobody is more determined to win this event than me."

I wanted to reestablish myself as a top-notch player who could still compete against the toughest competition in the world. I also believe that Robert Varkoni, who played excellent poker the entire tournament, had something to prove. As a highly underrated champion, he too wanted to gain some deserved respect from his peers. With that kind of motivation, I knew he would be tough to beat.

When I got heads-up with Robert, I had almost a 3 to 1 chip lead, yet I took nothing for granted and didn't think I had it locked up. I was proved all too right as he won a whole series of pots right off the bat with his aggressive play and almost got even with me in the chip count. I started to battle back, and then we played a huge pot that put him all in. He bet on a semibluff with a straight flush draw, but I had the top end of it blocked and had already made the nut straight, so he only had one out when he went all-in. When my hand held up, I was crowned the Champion of Champions, a title that I will cherish for the rest of my life.

The older lions of poker clearly dominated the final table. As I drove off in my shiny red Corvette, I saluted all us vintage champions with one last remark: "Old School Rocks!"

T.J.'S TALES
FROM TEXAS

When you've been on the road for as many years as T.J., you're bound to pick up a lot of stories along the way. Tales about the road gamblers, the tournament players, the big guys and the little guys, their bad beats and their big wins. Dramas with villains and heroes playing out their hands against the colorful backdrops of smoky backrooms and elegant casinos. Some of them faded the white line from Dallas to Houston while others made their marks on the big-time tournament circuit, each taking his cues from Lady Luck in the topsy-turvy world of poker.

On the next few pages, you'll read some of the good ol' boy stories that T.J. is famous for recounting to his many friends across the tables of poker rooms around the world.

JACK "TREETOP" STRAUS
AND HIS PRINCIPLE

Little Red Ashey and I were staying at the Anthony Motel in Hot Springs, Arkansas, while we were going to the horse races. "Let's go next door," says Little Red. "Jack Straus is there." So we went to the room next to us and had just started talking with Jack when we heard somebody pounding on the door. Jack opened the door and let a guy in.

You had to know Jack to understand this story. He borrowed and loaned a lot of money in his time, and it was always on what we called "principle." Principle meant that Jack set up a certain day to pay back his loan, and he only paid it on that exact day. Seems that Jack had borrowed $5,000 from this fellow and the guy had come over to dun him for the money. "I've still got thirty days to pay that off," Jack said, "so quit dunning me." And the guy left. As the first man was going down the stairs, a second man was coming up them. The door was still open so Jack let him in.

"I'm down on my luck," the man tells Jack. "Could you loan me $10,000?"

And Jack peeled the $10,000 right out of his pocket and gave it to him!

I couldn't explain Jack Straus any better than telling this story. This is the way he thought. One time when we were on the golf course, he told me that he liked me because I was like him. "I'm broke one day and have a fortune the next day," he said, "and I don't give a damn."

GEORGE MCGANN, ROBBER-PLAYER

George loved to play poker, but he was a stone killer. He stood about five foot eight or nine and weighed about 145 pounds, and he always wore a suit and tie. And he always carried two guns with him. One day George was playing at the AmVets in Dallas and he got broke. So he pulled out his gun and robbed everybody at the game, took every dime they had.

"Boys, I'm short," he says as he took their money.

But the kicker to this story is that the very next day, he came back into the game, sat down and played with these same guys—and nobody said a word!

Some years later when George was in his forties, he and his wife were murdered at the same time. The rumor was that he had been collecting money for somebody and somehow they had set him up.

Around Texas, they said that George had been accused of killing about thirty or forty people, but he was never actually convicted of murder.

TROY INMAN, THE PROTECTOR

The first time I went to Dallas to play poker, I played at the AmVets. I was playing with the great players in those days, guys like Bob Hooks, Kenny Smith, Dickie Carson, Bill Bonds and Bill Smith. It was a helluva no-limit hold'em game, and a tough guy named Troy Inman was running it.

I happened to win $8,000 the first time I played in it. When it came time for me to leave, I had to walk down three flights of stairs to get out of the place. And it was in a pretty bad area down in the lower Greenville section of Dallas near Highway 30. I got to wondering if I was gonna get out of the joint with all that money—Troy was pretty notorious for hiding around corners and shooting people and stuff like that.

As I was leaving, Troy says, "Wait a minute, T. J. With you packing that much cash on you, maybe I'd better walk down with you and be sure you get in your car."

So, he pulls out his pistol and we start walking down the stairs. I was more afraid of the guy protecting me than I was of having somebody from the outside rob me! But I got home with the money okay.

I'll tell you another story about Troy Inman. He was in and out of money. One time he left Dallas going to Shreveport and stopped off in Tyler, Texas, where he saw Henry Bowen, who had bought a house there. After he left Bowen's house, Troy went to a joint down on the river in Shreveport where they had a bunch of sexy girls doing the dancing—they weren't nude, they wore tops.

Anyway, he tipped off $1,000 in one night to these girls. They would come and sit with him at his table, and he'd give them $20 here, $20 there, and he'd give the head girl $40. But the kicker to the story is that he was broke at the time. He had stopped off in Tyler to borrow the $1,000 from Bowen!

A VERY UNLUCKY DAY IN ODESSA

A lot of people in Dallas were afraid of Troy. He had a sneaky reputation; you never knew what to expect from him. So, there was this card game one time in either Midland or Odessa, the site doesn't really matter. Nobody could play in this game except a bunch of notorious men from the area, the drug dealers and the bookmakers. And they were all what we called "packing" in Texas—they were all armed.

Seems that one guy accused another one of cheating, which they were all doing, and the guns started blazing. Two guys were killed right there in the game, and another guy was shot going out the front door.

All the houses were right next to each other, so the people next door heard all the gunshots and called for the cops. The man that was shot going out of the place started pounding on their door to ask for help, standing there just bleeding to death. The guy opened up the door and killed him with a shotgun, thinking that he was trying to break in.

That's one gambler who had a very unlucky day. Next time you think you're having a bad day in poker, just think about this guy!

CRAWFISH AND POKER IN BATON ROUGE

I was playing down in Baton Rouge years ago, where everything closes at 2:00 a.m. Across the bridge there was an all-night dance hall and restaurant that served great boiled crawfish on big tin platters. Right next to the dance hall, I noticed a door with a peephole drilled in it. I looked through it and saw a poker game going on, so I knocked on the door.

"Looks like a helluva game you're playin' in there," I said to the bouncer. "I've just got one question to ask you—if I happen to get lucky and win the money, can I get out of here with it?"

"In the five years I've been doing this job," he answered, "you're the first one who's ever asked me that question. I would suggest that you don't play."

So, I left. But most of the games that we played in around Texas were pretty secure and we never had any problems.

We played at Charlie Bissell's for eleven years and the police only raided us one time. It was a clean environment. He put on a brand new table top every two weeks, and he had the best food you've ever eaten in a poker game. Bissell ran a game with $5/$10/$25 blinds and at least once a week, we had $100,000 on the table. He would start out with a $5,000 buy-in, and if he lost one single quarter in the game, he would add another $5,000 to his stack, so there was always plenty of money to shoot at.

For $5, you could cut the cards. The way it worked was that if you put five bucks in the pot, you had the right to cut the deck before the next card was dealt. You could do this at any point in the game. Every time Charlie was on the draw, he always cut the cards, so you always knew where you stood with him.

THE POKER PLAYER WITH A SENSE OF HUMOR

Everett Goulsby was a famous man in Texas, and the way he acted in a poker game made him the funniest man I've ever seen at a poker table. He loved to brag so much that whenever he won a hand, he'd tell everybody around the table about it. We were playing down in Tyler one time and all the top players were there—Little Red Ashey, Bob Hooks, Cowboy Wolford, Johnny Wheeler. All the well-known players in Texas were playing, and Everett was winning pots.

George Lambert was running the game. He had a big gallon jug of booze sitting on the side of the table and he would take a sip or two before each hand. George was sitting on Everett's left and Johnny Wheeler sat to his right. Every time Everett won a pot, he would turn to Johnny and brag to him about how he had won that hand. And then George would reach over and take a $100 chip off of Everett's stack and put it in with his own. This happened every single time Everett won a hand. But the funniest part of the story is that everybody in the game except Everett saw it happen—and nobody ever told him!

Everett was a beaut. He made sure that he made an "appearance" every time we played poker. He'd wait to show up until about thirty minutes after the game started. He might have played with everybody in the game the day before, but he'd walk around the table and pat everybody on the back and say hello. But as soon as you beat him one time, he'd say, "You dirty so-and-so, you'll be broke and sleeping in the street and I'll still have money."

Everett was one of the best head-up players that ever played poker. The last time I saw him was just after he got out of jail from the twenty-two months that he did for bookmaking. "I'm just an old man now. I don't do anything anymore," he said to me. Part of his probation was that he couldn't go to Dallas County.

The last any of us heard about him, he had left the country because the cops were after him on other charges.

HEAD-UP AGAINST THE BEST

When you talk about the old timers who were great head-up players, the names Everett Goulsby and Jack Straus always come up. We used to say that if Everett's lips were moving, he was lying.

I went to him one time and asked, "How many times have you played Straus head-up?"

"I've played him three times and I beat him every time," he said. About a month later, I asked Jack the same question.

"I broke Everett all three times," he answered. So then, I had to figure out which one was telling the truth. Personally, I believed Straus.

Speaking of head-up play, I was at the World Series one year when Bobby Hoff was playing Betty Carey in a head-up match. This happened back when Dorfman, the multimillionaire from New York, was backing Betty. They were playing in the Sombrero Room at Binion's Horseshoe and they had at least $50,000 each on the table. On the first day they played, I saw Betty make a couple of draws on Bobby and vice versa. Bobby thought he was going to get to play her again the next day, but

Amarillo Slim cut in on him and played Betty and shut Bobby out of the game.

LITTLE RED AND FIVE-CARD STUD

Until just a few years ago, I thought that Little Red Ashey was the best card player I'd ever seen play—period, bar none—because of his judgment. He was about 6'5" tall and weighed almost three hundred pounds, had a deep voice and flaming red hair.

Little Red went to Tyler one evening to play in Lambert's game and I took a piece of him. Before the game started, he told me, "T. J., I'm gonna show you how to play tight today." And he did. If he had A-K in the first five seats, he wouldn't put the first quarter in. He won $3,800 in the game.

At one time, Little Red was rated as the best stud player in the United States. Five-card stud, not seven-card stud, was the game they played back then. A lot of people talk about Sarge Ferris being a great stud player. He and Little Red used to play in the same game with all the old timers in Shreveport, guys like Red Wynn, Corky McCorquodale, Slim Etheridge, Homer Marcotte, all the top five-card stud players were there. And Little Red was beating them all.

When he started coming to Vegas to play, Sarge would put up a bankroll for Ashey. "If anybody wants to play five-card stud," Sarge told him, "you go and play them. There's always money in the cage for you." But they only got it on a couple of times. George Huber tried it one time, and he didn't like it—he was supposed to be a good stud player, but he couldn't play Little Red.

Ashey also played hold'em as well as any man I've seen play the game. He had that rare judgment. He could lay down three of a kind one time, and then call you with a pair of fours the next time, and be right on both sides of the issue. Little Red is still around, but he doesn't play cards very much any more.

WHERE A LOT OF STORIES BEGIN AND END

They used to say in Dallas that a lot of stories begin and end with Everett Goulsby. Everett had what we call a real "sizz" factor. If he got stuck in a game, he was liable to play every hand for the next three hours. George Huber was staying with Everett at his house one time, so he drove George over to play in the game. Everett didn't want to play himself, but he took one-half of George's play.

Well, George got in the game for $2,000 and lost it all. Everett was sitting in the front room in his slippers and he says, "George, I'll show you how to play this game." George told Everett okay, but that he wanted twenty-five percent of him.

So Everett gets in the game and before long, he's in $26,000 with $8,000 left. I'm sitting in the game and we're down to five-handed with Everett sitting on my left. I had about $8,000 left, too. It was passed to me on the button and I look down at J-9 of clubs. So I made it $700 to go.

Everett was playing every hand and he just saddled right in for the $700. The flop came 10-8-7 of clubs! Everett moved in and I never had to make a bet. He had called with 10-7 offsuit and made two pair against my straight flush. And that was the end of him for that day.

Then just before they were leaving to go home, Everett goes over to George Huber and says, "Okay, George, you owe me twenty-five percent of $26,000."

"I'm only in for the first $1,000," George says. "And twenty-five percent of $1,000 is $250." Everett started steaming, and went home and threw George's suitcase on the lawn. That was the end of their relationship.

After I finished second in the Big One at the World Series in 1985, George called me in Dallas wanting to know if I'd loan him $2,000 to play the game in Houston. So I got the guys on the phone who were running the game and told them to give him the $2,000, that I'd be there in a few days to bring them the money. Later, I heard that George played two hands, cashed out his chips, and left with my money. And I haven't heard from him since.

KENNY "WHATTA PLAYER" SMITH

Kenny Smith was a big chess player in Texas and he just loved to play poker, played poker for years. He always wore a silk top hat that was supposed to have come from the theater where Abraham Lincoln was assassinated. He even had certification on it. Kenny would wear that hat in all the big tournaments, and every time he won a pot he would stand up from the table and yell, "Whatta player!" And that's how he got his nickname.

We were playing at the AmVets one time when Bob Hooks limped in and Ken Smith raised the pot up a pretty good amount of money. It came back to Hooks and he moved in his whole stack with two kings. Ken put the stall on Hooks for about three minutes, didn't look like he was ever going to act on his hand. So Hooks looks over and grabs Ken's cards out of his hand and sees two aces—and he moves Ken's chips into the pot himself! I'll bet that was the only time that Hooks ever lost a hand where he put the money in for himself and his opponent.

THE MYSTERY HAND PLAY

Bob Hooks was a great player who came in second one year at the World Series. He and I were playing in Shreveport one time when a play that I call my "mystery hand" came up. Wayne Edmunds was in the game with us and we were playing pot-limit hold'em. We'd been playing for quite a few hours and there was a lot of money on the table when a hand came up where I had the stone nuts on fourth street.

I had $5,000 in front of me and made a $2,000 bet. Wayne had a habit of putting his head down after he called a bet, so he never saw what was going on anywhere else at the table. As I was making my bet, the dealer grabbed my cards and threw them in the muck! Of course, Wayne didn't see it happen.

"What do I do now?" I was wondering. The dealer burned and turned the next card. I have big hands and I just kept them out in front of me like I was protecting my cards. I bet my last $3,000 and Wayne threw his hand away. I won the pot without any cards!

Bob and everybody else at the table except Wayne saw what happened, but nobody said a thing.

THE WORST BAD BEAT
OF ALL TIME

One year at the Bicycle Club, I was playing in a no-limit hold'em side game with Al Krux, a very fine player who has made several appearances at the final table at the World Series.

But Al wasn't doing very well in this game, and he was losing most of his money. He brought in the hand for his final money, $435. Two seats away there was a player who was holding his hand up in the air so that he could see it while a masseuse was giving him a rub down, and his opponent to his left could see it, too. This player decided not to call and threw his hand away.

It got around to me sitting just to the left of the dealer on the button, and I called the $435 with two tens. "This might be the best hand here," I thought, "since Al's all in and I can't lose any more than $435."

But the dealer didn't see that I had called and so she dropped the deck on the muck. She asked for a ruling and the floorman said that she had to reshuffle all of the cards except the two hands that Al and I were holding. The flop came K-10-4. Al had pocket kings and I had pocket tens. On fourth street came another 10, giving me four tens and winning the money against Al's full house.

But the kicker to this story is that the guy who had held his hand up before the flop had been dealt the two tens that came out on the flop after the reshuffle! The only way that I could possibly have a win against Al's hand was for the dealer to make a mistake, reshuffle those two tens back into the deck, and bring them back out again on the flop and fourth street. That ended Al's day—and I never won another pot that session. If you can think of a worse bad beat story than this one, I'd like to hear it!

SPEAKING OF BAD BEATS

Back in Texas there was a very famous poker player named Doc Ramsey, who couldn't stand to take a bad beat. He was the type of guy who would run around the room telling everybody what a bad beat he had taken and how he took it. If he saw you across the street walking the other way from him, he would cross the street just to tell you his bad-beat story.

One night he took a pretty bad beat and tried to tell everybody in the room about it, but nobody would listen to him.

"Doc," we said, "We've heard it a million times and we don't want to hear it again."

So he got up from the table, went into the kitchen, and cornered the Chinese chef. We all followed him and got a big kick out of watching him moaning to the chef, who didn't speak a word of English and just kept shaking his head as Doc rattled on.

MR. BROOKS AND THE TWO JACKS

Years ago in Dallas, Charlie Hendricks, a known gambler around Texas at the time, came to play with us in our no-limit game. In the old days, Bob Brooks had run all of the gaming in Anchorage, Alaska, but he had been playing in our Dallas game for several years and we had learned all of his moves. Everybody called him Mr. Brooks out of respect for his upstanding character.

He and Hendricks were playing in a five-way pot, and Mr. Brooks just flat called the preflop action from the little blind. Now it was time for Charlie to act from the big blind. He looked down and found two jacks in the hole.

"I can win this pot right now," he said to himself. "They've all limped in, so I'll just put in a raise because I've got the best hand." So he raised about $400. Everybody folded, and then it got around to Mr. Brooks in the little blind. He moved all-in.

Now Charlie thinks to himself, "I've gotta have the best hand. Mr. Brooks would never have passed a big hand there in the little blind." But we all knew Mr. Brooks. He was sitting there with pocket aces. He had been playing a trap the whole time and didn't care about just winning $25 from each person. He broke Charlie on this pot.

We were all laughing at the table, because it was the first time that Charlie had come to Dallas to play with us, and he didn't know how Mr. Brooks played. Nobody else on that table would have called with two jacks. It was very hard to get any money out of Mr. Brooks at the poker table.

One time when we were playing in a side game, I had two eights. I made a little token raise with them and Mr. Brooks and another player both called the raise. The flop came 8-8-4. When you flop quads, it is customary to check-check-check in the hope that somebody will catch up with you so that you can win a little something with the hand. But I decided to lead with the hand and bet $200 on the flop. Mr. Brooks called.

Fourth street brought a deuce. I bet $1,000 and he called that, too. On the end came a 10. I bet $2,500 and Mr. Brooks moved in on me. He had pocket tens and had filled on the river. That's one of the few times I ever won a big pot against him, about $10,000, and it all happened because I led at the pot with a huge hand.

If I had checked it all the way to the river, Mr. Brooks would have made a little bet on the end and I would have raised him. Then he would either have called me or made a small raise because there wouldn't have been enough money in the pot for him to put any real money in on the end. The way the hand worked out was just perfect for me.

THE BEST FEMALE POKER PLAYER IN THE WORLD

There has never been a woman poker player that could touch Betty Carey. She was the best female no-limit hold'em player I've ever seen. There were a lot of very good female limit hold'em and seven-card stud players at the time, but Betty was in a class by herself at no-limit. She took on all of the top players and played them head-up. Like Barbara Enright, she had a lot of guts.

Betty also had the biggest win anybody ever made at Bissell's—$51,000 in a $5/$10/$25 no-limit hold'em game one night. She had all the hands in the right spots and the guys weren't giving her credit for being the player that she was. She ate them alive. I was happy to get out of there even.

Betty was a consummate gambler. She gambled high, high, high. One night just after she'd arrived in Vegas, she walked into the Stardust while Dody Roach and I were shooting dice at the craps table. When she saw us, she just set her bags down by the table, and blew $60,000 before she even checked into the hotel. Dody was betting more than I was, and she was betting more than Dody. Yes, Betty was a gambler in the true sense of the word.

THE WORST DECISION IN THE HISTORY OF POKER

I was in tournament stress mode at a big tournament one year when something happened to me that shouldn't happen to a dog. I had never played the tournament before, but John Bonetti asked me to come out for it, so I was there for the last three days.

More than 400 players were in the limit-hold'em championship event, and we were down to six-handed play at the $2,000/$4,000 limits. I raised it up to $4,000 before the flop and it got around to the button. The guy on the button didn't see the raise and put in $2,000. The dealer reminded him that it was $4,000 to go since I had raised.

The button said, "Well, my hand isn't good enough for that," and grabbed back his $2,000. Then he threw his cards face down and they went into the muck, so that all you could see was the ends of his cards. The floorman was standing at the table and said to the dealer, "Don't kill that hand." So the dealer pulled the cards out of the muck and the floorman instructed the button to either leave the $2,000 in the pot and muck his hand, or put in the rest of the $4,000 and play out the hand. The button decided that rather than losing the $2,000, he would call with his K-J.

The flop came A-Q-10. He flopped the nut straight. I had A-K so, of course, I would have played the hand anyway six-handed. When the hand started, I had $12,000, and when it was over I had $2,000. Essentially, it cost me any chance of winning the event.

I didn't put up a fuss at the time, because I usually don't do that kind of thing. But when it was all over and I had been knocked out, I asked the floorman how he could have made a decision that allowed a player to pull cards out of the muck that were face down.

The tournament director excused the decision with, "Well, this is not the Horseshoe. We do things differently here."

Then I really got hot.

"Do you know how many times this has happened in a tournament with over 400 players, when people have put money in the pot and then pulled it back? Are you going to tell me that you made that decision every time?"

No, he couldn't see them every time.

"Then how could you have made that decision at a time when the big money is at stake?"

The only decision that could have been made was that the hand was dead when it touched the muck. Letting that hand live is the worst decision I've ever seen in a tournament.

THE TOUGHEST TABLE IN TOURNAMENT POKER

In the $5,000 tournament at the last Stairway to the Stars tournament that was held, the action got down to two tables, eighteen people. My starting table was probably the toughest table in the history of poker. There were Doyle Brunson, Chip Reese, Stu Ungar, Jack Keller, Berry Johnston, Dewey Tomko, David Baxter, Hamid Dastmalchi, and me. Among the nine of us, there were more than 150 tournament victories. The caliber of players was such that, if any one of us had made just the slightest error, he would have been gone.

The other table was full of unknowns, nobodies on the tournament circuit. When it got down to the final three, Hamid had the lead with $50,000 and Berry and I had about $25,000 each. Luckily, I won it. I seem to do better at tough tables because they tend to keep me in line.

Another tough tournament line-up happened at the Queens Classic $5,000 buy-in championship event in 1996. The final four were Doyle Brunson, Chip Reese, Eric Seidel, and me. This time, Doyle won it and I came in second. In the final hand, I held the A♠ 2♠ and he had a J-9 offsuit. The flop came A-J-9 with two spades, and we got it all in. Doyle's J-9 held up. As far as skill goes, this was the toughest final four I've ever come across.

19 A CONVERSATION WITH HALL OF FAMER, T.J. CLOUTIER

Dana Smith

If you ask players on the tournament circuit who they think are the best poker players in the world, T.J. Cloutier's name always comes up. Not because he's won the Big One— he hasn't yet, although he's come mighty close to winning it several times. And not because he's made the most money at the World Series—he hasn't, although he was the first player to make more than $1 million at it without winning the Main Event.

T.J. Cloutier's name is always mentioned because he is the player that they all respect and fear. He has won more than 60 big tournaments, has earned six gold bracelets at the World Series of Poker, and is a member of the Poker Hall of Fame.

His skills have been honed in the back rooms of Texas, in games where they were all carrying guns. His card sense was sharpened through years of beating the best of the road gamblers at no-limit hold'em. And his table demeanor has been polished on the rough surfaces of country roads as he faded the white line traveling to the next game.

T.J. is one of the last of the legendary road gamblers whose numbers are, unfortunately, dwindling each year. He brings a wealth of experience, card skill, and natural ability to every game that he plays. But more importantly, he always brings along his knowledge of the thousands of players that he has faced head-up in the decades that he has made his living as a professional poker player. And that sixth sense about what makes his opponents tick—that innate ability to put a player on a hand—is why his opponents fear him. It is as though he is looking at you through an invisible microscope, knowing what you are thinking, detecting your tells, delving into the inner spaces of your mind. You know that he knows you, knows what you're going to do next. And he's going to use his encyclopedic memory of how you play to beat you.

While T.J. and I were recording his life's story, I somehow had the feeling that I was sitting at the feet of a master, a master of people.

T.J. Cloutier graduated from Jefferson High School in Daly City, CA, where he was a three-letter man. At 6'3" tall, he was the center on the basketball team, played football, and still holds the home run record in baseball. And naturally, he was popular.

"When I was a senior, I dated Pat Kennedy, who later won the Miss California title," he modestly admits. "We had a study group of ten or fifteen kids that ran around together, and high school came very easy to me. It was when I got into college that I found out that you had to study."

T.J. entered the University of California at Berkeley on a baseball and football athletic scholarship, and played for Cal in the Rose Bowl in 1959 as a sophomore. But when his mother became ill, he dropped out of college to go to work and help his father pay some of her medical bills. Then the army snapped him up, since he no longer was a draft-deferred student.

He gained his first experience playing poker when he was a caddy at the Lake Merced and San Francisco Country Clubs. One day, somebody passed around some "lucky bucks" from Artichoke Joe's, a cardroom in San Francisco. For $15, he received a $20 buy-in for the lowball game. So, at the age of seventeen years, T.J. started playing poker in a public cardroom and by the time he was nineteen years old, he was playing head-up draw poker against Artichoke Joe himself.

"When I began playing, all the games were no-limit, including no-limit lowball without the joker and no-limit high draw poker," he reflects. "Then when I entered college, I played poker at the Kappa Alpha house with Joe Capp, the Cal quarterback who later played in the NFL, and Bobby Gonzalez, who became a supervisor in San Francisco. I found out that I had a knack for the game, although I lost everything I had at the time. Actually, I was honing my skills at observation and getting to know people. I've always had a sort of photographic memory for how people play their hands in certain situations. If you and I had played poker together five years ago, I wouldn't remember your name, but I would remember your face and how you played your hands in different situations, your tendencies. It's a visual memory thing, like pages opening up in a book in my mind. I've always been very observant throughout my entire life."

When T.J. got out of the army, where he furthered his training at poker, he walked into the office of the Montreal Allouettes and asked to try out with them. He went to one workout and made the team, after not having played any football for two years. The team paid his expenses until the training camp began, and he played first string tight end for the Allouettes until he was traded to the Toronto Argonauts. Thirteen Americans were suited up, along with seventeen Canadians.

"My value was that my father was born in Canada, so I could play as a Canadian—an American-trained Canadian was just what they were looking for. It's a rugged brand of football, wide open. When I was playing, you couldn't block for a pass receiver once he caught the ball past the line of scrimmage. The field was 110 yards long, the end zones were twenty yards deep, and the field was wider. You had to make a first down in the first two downs or else kick the ball, since there were only three downs. It was a real fast game, and everybody was in motion all the time.

"You couldn't block for a punt receiver; once you caught the ball, you were on your own. You had to give the punt receiver five yards to catch the ball. So, the other team would circle him like the Indians circling the settlers, and as soon as he caught that ball, he was dead, flatter than a pancake."

T.J. played Canadian football for five years, until his knees gave out. Then he received a call from Victoria when they were trying to form the Continental Football League. Victoria offered him its coaching job, but he also would have to play. "Are you kidding?" he asked. "If I could still play, I'd be playing for Montreal or Toronto."

When he left Canada, T.J., his father, and his brother-in-law started Bets Quality Foods, an acronym for Bill, Ed, and Tom (T.J.'s first name), and later brought T.J.'s brother in with them.

"We used the money I had left from football and my dad's retirement to start the business. Our slogan was 'Your Best Bet in Quality Foods.' We bought a huge freezer from Foster's, a big cafeteria chain in San Francisco, when they went out of business and rebuilt it in our warehouse to handle our frozen food. We had a big egg business, too, although you don't make much money from eggs. But when you're serving big hotels, you have to give them the eggs at a good price to keep their other business. I was working 16 hours a day—I would take orders, load trucks, and pick up and deliver products. Later, we merged with A & A Foods, and they stole us blind. My dad won an 11-count court case against them, but the owners left the country and he never got a nickel."

After suffering this bad beat, T.J. began delivering bread for Toscana and eventually wound up as night manager for Wonder Bread in San Francisco.

"My first wife and I split up about that time, and I ended up heading for Texas with $100 in my pocket. That was in 1976. I went to work for six months as a derrick man on the oil rigs down there. On my off days, I was playing poker. Pretty soon, I was making more money at poker than I was on the rigs. I'd been freezing up there anyway, so that's how I moved into playing poker full time."

He played no-limit hold'em in Longview and pot-limit hold'em in Shreveport, fifty-one miles away. The games in Shreveport were so good, T.J. moved there to play poker every day at the Turf Club. "The games were much smaller than we're playing now. On Sundays, they would have a big game run by an old gambler named Harlan Dean who was well known in all the gambling places. He used to be George Barnes' partner in the bridge tournaments in Vegas, and he was one of the original hold'em players.

"I ended up selling the chips, and if I got broke or something, he'd call up on a Sunday and ask, 'Well, we're broke, are we, ol' partner?' And I'd say, 'Well, Mr. Dean, I know you're not broke, but I am.' Then he'd say, 'Well, you come on by today and I'll give you some chips.' And if I got loser in the game, I could have the chip rack because he didn't want the game to end. That's when I started playing real serious poker."

While T.J. was living in Shreveport, he played poker every day. "In fact," he said, "I was having a gay old time. I was single then, and would go to the Louisiana Downs 100 out of the 105 days of the meet, and then go out and play poker every night.

I learned more about poker in Shreveport than anywhere else in the world.

"There was a real good game on Sunday and Jim "Little Red" Ashey used to play in it. He's bigger than I am—about 6'5" tall and 300 pounds—but everybody called him Little Red because he started playing there when he was about sixteen or seventeen years old. I learned more from just watching him play than any other way, and then suiting those moves to my own style, which was aggressive at times and passive at other times. You can't let them pigeonhole you, you know.

"A lot of people think that Sarge Ferris was the best five-card stud player in the world. But when Red was seventeen years old, he was playing with Sarge, Corky McCorquodale, Homer Marcotte—all the big names in five-card stud used to play in Shreveport. And Little Red beat them all the time.

"Wherever Homer Marcotte went, he would say, 'I'm the Louisiana Man!' He was shot dead by some guy about 5'5" tall in a Dallas bar back around 1978 over a $50 bar bill. The little guy kept dunning Marcotte for the $50 and Homer kept saying, 'Don't you know me? I'm the Louisiana Man. You don't dun me for $50.' Finally, this little guy had heard enough, went out to his car to get his gun, came back in, and shot Marcotte.

"Anyway, when Sarge went out to Vegas and won all that money, he put up a bankroll for Red while the World Series was on so that if Red came out, he'd have the money to play against anybody that wanted to play him. The only person I know of that they ever got a game on with was George Huber, and he didn't last two hours against Red. Lost about $40,000 to him. Of course, Red didn't come out very often because he hated to fly. You'd almost have to give him a shot like Mister T on the old A-Team show just to get him on an airplane. Red liked horses and sports betting, so all his money went there, and poker wasn't fast enough for him anymore."

In 1978, T.J. made his first trip to the World Series of Poker, although he didn't play in the championship tournament until 1983 (the year that Tom McEvoy won it). But in 1985, the third year that he played in the Main Event, he finished second to Bill Smith, with Berry Johnston taking third.

"When it got down to three-handed, Berry Johnston had the best hand, an A-K. I had an A-J. The flop came K-J-little, and we got it all in. On the turn, I caught a jack and drew out on him to put him out of the tournament. Then it got to two-handed and I had the lead against Bill. But the key hand of the whole match happened when I had two nines and he had two kings. He moved in and I called him with my nines. He won the pot and doubled up. Then he had a big lead, and I started chopping back at him.

"There were 140 players that year, so there was $1,400,000 in chips. I got back to $350,000, and then Bill came in with a little raise. I looked at an ace in my hand didn't even look at the other card, but made it look like I had. I just went over the top of him with the whole $350,000. I knew that Bill had to make a decision—if he made the wrong one, I'd be back even with him again. He had started drinking, and he gave away money when he was drinking. He called. When I looked back at my hand, my kicker was a three. And Bill had two threes. They held up and he won the title.

"He was one of the greatest players of all time, Bill Smith was. Bill was the tightest player you'd ever played in your life when he was sober. And when he was halfway drunk, he was the best player I'd ever played with. But when he got past that halfway mark, he was the worst player I'd ever played with. And you could always tell when he was past the halfway point because he started calling the flop. Say a flop came 7-4-10—he would say, '21!' or some other remark like that. When he got up to take a walk, he would have a little hop in his step, a 'git up in his gittalong' we used to call it. And then you knew he was gone. But Bill had such great timing on his hands when he was younger and wasn't drunk, he was out of this world. He'd make some fabulous plays, plays you couldn't believe. He was a truly great player."

A lot of good hold'em players came from the South, from the Sun Belt states. T.J. is one of the best of them. "While I was living in Shreveport, I found out about a real good game in Dallas that was run by a man that I will call the 'Big Texan.' It was a $5/$10/$25 no-limit hold'em game with either a $500 or a $1,000 buy in. I used to drive the two hundred miles from Shreveport three days a week to play in that game."

The first twelve times that he played in the game, he won. Then, on his next visit, the Big Texan told T.J. that he was "dropping the latch" on him, that T.J. had to give him half of his play or he couldn't play there anymore. So, T.J. gave him half his action for his next ten visits—and he won all ten times.

"Then one day I went down there and out of the blue, the Big Texan said to me, 'I'm out today.' That rang a warning bell in my head. I knew there was something going on, something was wrong. I noticed two new players in the game, so I just bought in for $500 in chips, played for about an hour, and hardly ever got into a pot. Then I left."

That was around the time that Bill Smith and T.J. became friends. Bill's wife, Cleta, was working at Mitsubishi Aircraft in New Orleans and introduced T.J. to Joy, whom he married in 1984. "That's the reason I moved to Dallas from Shreveport, not just because of the game but because Joy lived there. She was the personal secretary to the president of Mitsubishi." Today, Joy travels with T.J. to most of the tournaments on the circuit.

T.J.'s play at the World Series of Poker is always open to Lyle Berman, his first major tournament backer. "Lyle doesn't get to many tournaments anymore, but he always makes it to the WSOP. As high as you've ever heard of in a poker game, Lyle plays it. He plays in the high games with Doyle and the others. He's one of the two or three people that play in that game who can really afford it. But that's not it: He's a great card player, a brilliant poker player. He has no fear whatsoever, no matter how much you bet at him.

"In fact, in the final game that he and Bob Stupak played before Bob's Stratosphere project was completed, Stupak brought it in for $25,000. They were playing no-limit deuce-to-seven with no cap. Usually, they played with a $75,000 cap, which means that you can't lose more than $75,000 on one hand, but that night they were playing the game with no cap. Lyle called the bet with 2-3-5-7, drawing at the deuce-to-seven wheel. He drew one card while Stupak stood pat. When all the shouting was over, Stupak had bet $390,000 on his hand, an 8-5 pat, which is a great hand in deuce-to-seven. But Lyle caught a 6 and made a 7 on Stupak to win the pot. From what I understand, Stupak still owes Lyle some of that money."

T.J. has won six World Series titles. In fact, he was the first man to earn $1 million at the Series without winning the Main Event. When I asked which year he won the limit Omaha title, he said, "I'd have to go look at my bracelet. I've won over fifty titles and I can't keep them all straight. The only major tournament where I haven't won the big title so far is the World Series, but I came in second to Bill Smith and placed fifth to Chan the year that he beat Erik Seidel for the championship. And, of course, I came second to Ferguson in 2000."

That was his biggest tournament disappointment. After starting the final table in last chip position, T.J. inched his way up the chip ladder and finally drew even with Ferguson, the overwhelming chip leader at the start of the day. On the last hand of the tournament, T.J. raised all in with an A-Q and Ferguson called with an A-9. Ferguson won the title when he rivered a 9.

"I won the last $5,000 tournament held at the Stardust, the Stairway to the Stars. That also was the year that I won the last Diamond Jim Brady tournament at the Bicycle Club, and I told them before it started, 'I won the last one at the Stairway to the Stars, I won the last one at the Union Plaza, I won the last one at the Frontier—this place might blow up next week if I win the big one here, too.' I wound up winning the Bike's Diamond Jim Brady tournament three years in a row. That was sort of a peak for me that I don't think can ever be repeated.

"The first year that I won the Diamond Jim Brady, Mansour Matloubi and I started head-up play with about even chips. I had played with him for about five hours that day at the final table and he never ran a bluff on anybody one time, not once. He wanted to get down to the final two. When we got head-up, he bet me $120,000 on the final hand, and I called him with third pair in a New York split second because I knew that I had the best hand. I'd been chipping away at him so bad that he decided to try to run a big bluff on me. And that was the end of it.

"Then when Tuna Lund and I got head-up the next year at the Diamond Jim Brady, Tuna had $360,000 and I had $120,000. I chipped away at him and chipped away at him and chipped away at him. Finally, he made a $50,000 bet on the end on one hand and I called him with a pair of nines. He said, 'You got me.' And I answered, 'Wait a minute. Before you show your hand, I'll bet you have a Q-10 offsuit.' He turned it over and sure enough, that's what he had. That was the key hand.

"The third year I won the Diamond Jim Brady, it got down to Bobby Hoff and me, so I played a formidable player every year. But in this one, I had three to one chips on Hoff, not like the second year that I played when I came into the second day of the tournament with the low chips. The key hand that year was when I had two nines against Hal Kant's two eights, which doubled me up from $9,000 to $18,000 and then I just went from there."

While T.J. is competing in a tournament, he sometimes plays cash games, although there are times when he doesn't play any side action at all. He also occasionally plays in the satellites. "At the Hall of Fame, I had a run one year when I played in six super satellites and got a seat in four of them, and I played in six one-table satellites and won four of those. So, I won close to $35,000 on the side in the satellites.

"You get some pretty weak fields in satellites, although at the Big One they're not usually as weak as they are for some of the other tournaments. In a $10,000 satellite, you get $2,000 in chips so you can play the game. But you have only $200 or $300 in chips in the megasatellites, so everybody's just moving in all the time and you'll get drawn out on a lot. If you only have that many chips, all of them are in jeopardy the first round that you play. Or you'll try to draw out on somebody else, whereas you wouldn't try to do that with a big stack. One year, I played in a $10,000 satellite at the Golden Nugget and five people moved in all of their chips on the first hand. So one guy ended up with $10,000 in chips after the first hand."

The thing that has made T.J. so successful at no-limit and pot-limit hold'em is his observation powers. "I know what Joe Blow is going to do in this situation and in that situation. That's what helps me. When I'm in a tournament with all strangers, after fifteen or twenty minutes I'm going to know how they play. Say what you want, but there are people who have that ability, and there are people who don't have it. You're either born with it or you aren't. I have a knack for picking up people's tells and all the little things that they do. Caro has a book on tells, but I have my own book.

"One time in the World Series I had two kings twice during the first two hours of the $10,000 championship tournament. Both times, I made a little raise and was reraised, and I threw the kings away before the flop. And both times, I was right: Mike Allen showed me aces on both hands. I knew the player and so I knew the kings weren't any good. It's very hard to lay down two kings; it's easier to play queens because you can get away from them easier than you can two kings.

"But then, I remember a time when I blew it at the Hall of Fame. There was one guy at the table that I didn't know. It was the first hand that was dealt and I was in the big blind with the K-9 of diamonds in an unraised pot. The flop came 7-2-3 of diamonds. This guy led off and bet from the number one seat, the fellow on the button called, and I raised right there. The guy in the one-seat moved all in, and the man on the button (who had turned a set) called. Ordinarily, I would have thrown away my hand. The only player that I didn't know was the guy who moved all in, and he had the A-J of diamonds in his hand. So, I went broke on the hand and went out first in that tournament."

Do beats like that cause players to steam?

"No, I never steam. I might steam on the inside, but I never let other players see it. But I remember one time when Phil Hellmuth got knocked out of the Diamond Jim Brady tournament. A velvet rope was connected to two poles at each door so that people couldn't wander into the room. Phil went on a dead sprint and tried to leap over that rope, caught his foot on it, and went sprawling out into the room.

"Another time during a limit hold'em tournament at the Diamond Jim Brady, the whole room was completely packed, and you know how much noise there is in a tournament room like that. A mulatto girl came into the room wearing a dress with cross hatches down the back of it cut all the way down, real low. She was an absolutely beautiful woman. She walked over to talk with Jerry Buss, and the whole room went silent, totally silent. When she finished talking with Jerry, the entire room started clapping, right in the middle of the tournament.

"In contrast, I was playing a tournament at the Normandie Casino one time when I saw an older lady pick up her cards to look at them up close, had a heart attack, and keeled over dead. The two tables around her caused some commotion, but the other tables didn't even stop playing, nobody even noticed. But this gorgeous girl had stopped play in the whole room!"

Do players prepare for tournaments?

"When I'm taking my shower in the morning, I think about a few things, devise a plan. Then my wife, who's with me most of the time, gives me a kiss and says, 'I love you and good luck.' Then she says, 'Now, concentrate and don't do anything foolish. Catch some cards.' It's the same thing each time."

T.J. also plays in tournaments other than no-limit and pot-limit hold'em, including seven-card stud, Omaha, Omaha high-low split and lowball. "I never used to play stud tournaments, because being from Texas and seeing what things can be done with a deck, I never liked a game where the same person always gets the first card like they do in stud. I've run into enough cheats and mechanics in my lifetime who could win every pot if the right guy was dealing. And, of course, most of the players in a stud tournament play the game every day, so I wouldn't play in one. But I was playing at Foxwoods a few years ago and Phil Hellmuth, my backer at the time, talked me into playing the $5,000 satellite for the seven-card stud tournament. I won it, and went on to finish fourth in the tournament. Then he insisted that I play all the stud events. So, in the first twelve stud tournaments I played, I won one, had two seconds, two thirds, and a fourth-place finish. I no longer feel unkindly toward stud. Besides, I know there's nothing going on in stud tournaments like there used to be in some of the ring games.

"Except for the year that Larry Flynt played in the tournament at Binion's when he tried to buy off the table. He had a big bet with Doyle, something like $1 million to $10,000 that Larry couldn't win the tournament. When it got down to three or four tables, Larry tried to buy off some of the players and actually did buy off some of them by getting them to throw off their chips to him. But Jack Binion had gotten wind of it and he had Dewey Tomko watching the table for him from the side. He saw what was going on, and Larry Flynt was never allowed to come back and play in the WSOP. Of course, none of this poker stuff was in the movie about Flynt."

T.J. has opened up his repertoire to include Omaha and Omaha high-low split, games that are so different from no-limit hold'em, and has a bracelet in each form of Omaha. He explains his success this way: "Tournaments are tournaments. You use the same process in every game; you work yourself up to the final table. Final table play is the same, no matter what the game is. So, if you have a knack for playing the final table, you have a chance to win. I know a lot of players who can get to the last table, but very few of them know how to play it once they get there."

Is it difficult to maintain a stable relationship when you play poker professionally?

"My poker playing is my job, and I separate it from my life outside the poker room. I cannot understand people who can play poker three or four days in a row and then can't wait to get right back to it again; they don't have any other life. I used to play steady in Dallas, five days a week, strictly no-limit hold'em against the best players in the world. Players used to come from Vegas and everywhere else to play in that game.

"At least once a week, we had over $100,000 on the table. This game was played every Monday, Wednesday, and Friday; there was another game that was played on Tuesdays and Thursdays. You could play at noon every day, and then again at 7:00 that night. So, I would play until 5:00 each night, go see a movie, and then go play the evening game, unless the first game was so good that I didn't want to leave it. I followed that schedule for years and I never played on the weekends. When poker is your profession, you treat it like a job. But for some players, poker not only is their job, it's their hobby as well. You need some balance."

When they are at their home in Dallas, T.J. enjoys golfing at the country club and then meeting his wife for dinner after he leaves the greens. She likes antiquing and taking care of their home.

"Joy is my support. She always sits in the background when I'm in a tournament. She's right there and she knows that I know she's there. I look over and smile at her, or if I've lost a hand, I'll make a little expression that she recognizes. She doesn't know anything about poker, but she knows that if I move all of my chips in and then get the pot back, I've won; and if I don't, I've lost. She does all the book work and takes care of the business end of things."

When he and Joy went on their honeymoon, they spent a few days in New Orleans. While Joy went antiquing, T.J. went to the track and won $5,000 on the horses. From there, they traveled to Tampa where they went to the dog races and he won another $3,800. "After all our expenses were paid, we came home $5,000 ahead," he laughed.

In what other profession in the world, I thought, can you go out for an evening's dinner and entertainment, play some poker along the way, and come home with more money than you started with? "Yes," T.J. commented, "but in what other profession can you work all day long and come home losing for the day?!"

Considering that he is one of the most feared players on the tournament circuit, T.J. actually comes across as being quite modest about his accomplishments. "I wouldn't say that I'm modest, but I'm not the type to go around saying, 'I'm the Louisiana Man.' I feel in my own bones that I can play with anyone, and I don't fear anybody alive."

That feeling of confidence without the baggage of ego involvement may be the combination that gives T.J. his edge at the poker table. Like so many poker players and tournament winners I've interviewed, T.J. admits that he doesn't have that same edge in every gambling game he plays. Even the best have a few leaks in their gaming activities.

"I've had a lot of holes that I've tried to patch up. I love craps and over the years, I've lost a lot of money at it. I used to love to run to the crap table all the time and, of course, that hurts your side play because it's so much faster than the poker. But now if I play craps, I go to the table with only a limited amount of money, no ATM card, nothing like that. I've made several scores of over $50,000 off of $500—but if I go to the table with $20,000 I don't win a single bet!"

It's just another of the lessons that T.J. has learned throughout his career. The rest of them, he has down pat.

GLOSSARY

Any ace

An ace with a weak kicker. "Sure, you can win any ace just like Jack did with his A-7, but in the long run you'll lose money because you've got no kicker."

Backdoor a flush/straight

Make a hand that you were not originally drawing to by catching favorable cards on later streets. "I had been betting top pair, but when a fourth spade hit at the river, I *backdoored* a flush."

Backup

A card that provides you with an extra out. "If you have a drawing hand, you like to have a *backup* to your draw, a secondary draw that might make your hand the winner."

Beat into the pot

When an opponent bets an inferior hand, you gladly—and quickly—push your chips into the pot. "When three clubs came on the flop, Slim moved in. I *beat him into the pot* with my flush—he had a 10-high flush, mine was higher."

Behind

Other players will have to act before you do. "So long as you're sitting *behind* the other players, you have the advantage of position."

Big ace

An ace with a big kicker (A-K or A-Q). "When the flop came A-6-2, I played my *big ace* strong."

Big flop

The flop comes with cards that greatly enhance the strength of your hand. "I caught a *big flop* that gave me the nut flush."

Boss hand

A hand that is the best possible hand. "When you have the *boss hand*, you should bet it as aggressively as possible, especially if you think your opponents have drawing hands."

Broken board

The board cards are random with no pair and no flush or straight possibilities. "A *broken board* such as 9-5-2 is a fabulous flop to pocket jacks."

Bully

Play aggressively. "When I have a big stack in a tournament, I like being able to *bully* the entire table."

Change gears

Adjust your style of play from fast to slow, from loose to tight, from raising to calling, and so on. "When the cards quit coming his way, Will didn't *change gears*; instead, he kept on playing fast and lost his whole bankroll."

Cold call

Call a raise without having put an initial bet into the pot. "Bonetti raised, Hellmuth reraised, and I *cold called*."

Come over the top

Raise or reraise. "I raised it $2,000 and Sexton *came over the top* of me with $7,000."

Commit fully

Put in as many chips as necessary to play your hand to the river, even if they are your case chips. "If I think the odds are in my favor, I will *fully commit*."

Decision hand

A hand that requires you to make a value judgment. "The great hands and the trash hands play themselves. It is the *decision hand* that will determine your profit at the end of the session, the day, the year. It is all of the marginal, in-between hands that are played with great ability that separate winners from losers."

Flat call

You call a bet without raising. "When he bet in to me, I just *flat called* to keep the players behind me from folding."

Flop to it

The flop enhances the value of your hand. "If you don't *flop to it*, you can get away from the hand."

Get into the deck

Get a free card. "If you just check your one-pair hand, you allow your opponents to *get into the deck*."

Get away from it

To fold what appeared to be a winning hand until an unfavorable flop negated its potential. "If you don't flop to your hand, *get away from* it."

Get the right price

The pot odds are favorable enough for you to justify calling a bet or a raise with a drawing hand. "Since I was getting the *right price*, I called the bet with a wraparound."

Get full value

Bet, raise and reraise to manipulate the size of the pot so that you will win the maximum number of chips if you win the hand. "By raising on every round, I was able to get *full value* when my hand held up at the river."

Get there

You make your hand. "When you *get there*, you might be able to start maximizing your bets."

Give them

You attribute a hand to your opponents. "When the flop comes with a pair and your opponent raises, what are you going to *give him*, a straight draw?"

Gone goose

You're a beaten player. "When an ace hit on the flop, I figured that I was a *gone goose* with my king."

Isolate

You raise or reraise to limit the action to yourself and a single opponent. "I raised on the button to *isolate* against the big blind."

Jammed pot

The pot has been raised the maximum number of times and may also be multiway. "You should pass with a weak hand if the pot has been *jammed* before it gets to you."

Key card

The one card that will make your hand a winner. "I knew that I needed to catch a 10, the *key card* to my straight draw."

Lay it down

Fold. "Many times, you can put enough pressure on the pot to blow everybody away and sometimes even get the raiser to *lay down* his hand."

Limp

Enter the pot by just calling rather than raising. "You might decide to just *limp* in with a pair of tens and see the flop as cheap as possible."

Limper

A player who enters the pot for the minimum bet. "With two *limpers* in the pot, a pair of jacks should be your minimum raising hand."

(Two) Limper rule

Once two or more people have voluntarily entered the pot for the minimum bet, the pot already has shaped up to be multiway. "Small pairs and connectors become somewhat more attractive in middle to late position when *two or more players have limped* into the pot in front of you."

Live cards

Cards that you need to improve your hand and which probably are still available to you. "When three players who I knew to be big-pair players entered the pot in front of me, I thought that my middle connectors might still be *live* so I decided to play the hand."

Live one

A loose, inexperienced or bad player. "Very seldom do you get a *live one*, a person who can't play at all, in the big games but it does happen sometimes."

Long call

Take a long time to decide whether to call a bet with a marginal hand. "When you're studying whether to call, making a *long call*, your opponents can get a read on you."

Make a move

Try to bluff. "When the board paired sixes, Max *made a move* at the pot. I thought he was bluffing but I had nothing to call him with."

Middle buster

An inside straight draw. "If the flop comes A-10-4 and you have the Q-J, you're not going to draw to the *middle buster* to try to catch the king."

Nit and Supernit

A very tight player and a supertight player. "The *nit* is a person who plays tight and takes no chances. The *supernit* will drive from one county to the other, win one pot, quit the game and drive home."

(the) Nut draw

You have a draw to the best possible hand. "When two clubs come on the board and you have the A§J§, you have the *nut* flush *draw*."

(the) Nuts

The best hand possible at the moment. "Remember that you can flop the *nuts* and lose it on the turn; for example, when you flop the nut straight and the board pairs making a full house for your opponent."

Nutted up

When someone is playing very tight. "Jackson was so *nutted up* at the final table, I stole pot after pot from him."

Out (an)

A card that completes your hand. "Always try to have an extra *out*, a third low card to go with your ace, when you're drawing for the low end."

Overpair

You have a pair in your hand that is higher than the highest card showing on the board. "When the board came Q-J-6, I flopped an *overpair* with my pocket kings."

Pay off

You call an opponent's bet at the river even though you think that he might have the best hand. "When the board paired at the river, I decided to *pay him off* when he bet because I wasn't sure that he had made trips."

Peddling the nuts

Drawing to, playing and betting the nut hand. "Players may not always be peddling the nuts in a heads-up situation, but in any multiway pot somebody's usually drawing at the nuts if he doesn't already have it."

Piece of cheese

A hand that is a loser. "If you raise and get reraised, your trip threes are probably *a piece of cheese*, so be very careful when you flop bottom set."

Play back

Responding to an opponent's bet by either raising or reraising. "If a tight opponent *plays back* at you, you know he probably has the nuts."

Play from behind

Checking with the intent of check-raising when you have a big hand. "I knew that Kevin usually *played from behind* when he had a big hand so when he checked, so did I."

Play fast

Aggressively betting a hand to get full value for it if you make it. "Many players *play fast* in the early rounds of rebuy tournaments to try to build their stacks."

Play slow

The opposite of playing fast; waiting to see what develops before pushing a hand. "When you make the nut straight on the flop and there's a chance that the flush draw is out or possibly a set, why not play your hand *slow* to start with?"

Play with

Staying in the hand by betting, calling, raising or reraising. "You should realize that you're going to *get played with* most of the time because hold'em is a limit-structure game."

Put on the heat

Pressure your opponents with aggressive betting strategies to get the most value from your hand. "You might consider *putting on the heat* when your opponent is slightly conservative or when he has a short stack against your big stack."

Put pressure on the pot

Bet aggressively to make it expensive for opponents to play. "If you don't want Loose Larry to draw to his straight, you have to continually put pressure on the pot."

Put them on (a hand)

You assign a value to your opponent's hand. "Using my instincts and the way he had played the hand, I *put Stanley on* the nut low."

Rag (or blank)

A board card that doesn't help you and appears not to have helped anyone else, either. "The flop came with A-2-3 and then a *rag*, the 9ª, hit on the turn."

Rag off

The river card doesn't help you. "Then it *ragged off* on the end and he was a gone goose for all his money."

Rainbow flop

The flop cards are three different suits. "I liked my straight draw when the flop came *rainbow* and nobody could have a flush draw against me."

Rake game

Money taken out of a pot by the house as its fee for running a game. "In the very lowest limit games, it's hard to come out ahead because of the rake extracted from each pot."

Read the board

Understand the value of your hand in relation to the cards on the board. "If you *read the board* correctly, you often can tell where you're at in the hand by the action."

Rock

A very conservative player who always waits for premium cards before he plays a hand. "Smith was playing like a *rock* so when she bet into me, I knew she had me beat."

Run over

Playing aggressively in an attempt to control the other players. "If they're not trying to stop you from being a bully, then keep *running over them* until they do."

Runner-runner

Catch cards on the turn and river that make your hand a winner. "As it turns out, you had a suited K-J, caught *runner-runner* to make a flush, and broke me!"

Showdown

When the cards are turned over at the river to determine the winner after all betting has been completed. "If everyone checks to you at the river and you couldn't win in a *showdown*, why bet if you know that you will get called?"

Shut down

Discontinue aggressive action. "When the board paired the second highest card, I decided to *shut down*."

Slowplay

You intentionally do not bet a strong hand for maximum value because you are hoping to trap your opponents. "I knew the rock in the third seat was *slowplaying* aces so I didn't bet my kings when he checked on the flop."

Smooth call

Call a bet without raising. "If someone bets into you, you might *smooth call* with this type of hand."

Stand a raise

Call a raise. "I recently *stood a raise* in a cash game with 9-8 on the button. The board came 7-6-2, no suits. A guy led off with a decent bet and I called him with my overcards and a straight draw."

Stiffed in

Play a blind hand in an unraised pot. "The only time that you might play 7-2 in hold'em is when you are *stiffed in* in the big blind."

Surrender

Give up on your hand. Fold. "When the fourth flush card hit at the river, I had to *surrender*."

Take off a card

Call a bet on the flop. "I decided to *take off a card* and see what the turn would bring."

Takeoff hand

A hand that has the potential of beating a better starting hand because it is live. "In four-way action, I figured that my middle connectors might turn into a *takeoff hand*."

Take them off (a hand)

Beat a superior starting hand. "Any of those types of hands in which you have two straight cards and a pair will *take the aces right off* a lot of times."

Three bet

A bet and two raises. "Daugherty bet, McEvoy raised and Cloutier made it three bets."

Time game

A game in which the house collects a fee from players at regular intervals. "Every half-hour the Central Casino collects $5 from each player in its time games."

Top pair top kicker

In hold'em, one of your pocket cards combines with the highest board card to make a pair, and your side card is the highest possible backup card. "When the board came K-J-9-6-2, Tom's A-K gave him top pair top kicker."

Underpair

You hold a pair that is lower than a pair showing on the board. "Why would you ever want to call with an *underpair*?"

Wake up with a hand

You are dealt a hand with winning potential. "Just because a player is a maniac doesn't mean that he can't *wake up with a hand.* Over the long haul, everybody gets the same number of good hands and bad hands."

Weak ace

You have an ace in your hand but you do not have a high kicker to go with it. "I won't bet a *weak ace* unless I am certain that I have the only ace at the table."

Where you're at

You understand the value of your hand in relation to the other players' hands. "Your opponent may not know for sure *where you're at* in the hand when you have played it in a deceptive way."

World's fair

A big hand. "Suppose the flop comes 8-8-4, no suits. You know you're up against either nothing or *the world's fair.*"